The York Grand Lodge

David Harrison

To Helen

Sometimes I seem to see thee rise
A glorious child again —
All virtues beaming from thine eyes
That ever honoured men —
Emily Jane Brontë

Published 2014 by arima publishing

www.arimapublishing.com

ISBN 978 1 84549 629 6

© David Harrison 2014

Printed and bound in the United Kingdom

Typeset in Garamond

arima publishing

ASK House, Northgate Avenue

Bury St Edmunds, Suffolk IP32 6BB

t: (+44) 01284 700321

www.arimapublishing.com

Contents

Map of Yorkshire

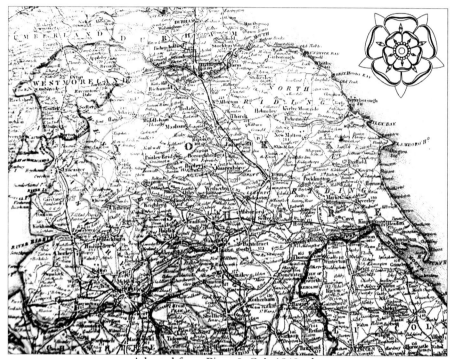

Adapted from Pigot & Co's 1840 atlas

Abbreviations

AQC   Transactions of the Ars Quatuor Coronatorum

DCRO   Durham County Record Office

JCRFF   The Journal for the Centre of Research into Freemasonry and
        Fraternalism

JIVR   The Journal of the Institute of Volunteering Research

LCHS   The Transactions of the Lancashire and Cheshire Historical Society

THSLC   Transactions of the Historic Society of Lancashire and Cheshire

UGLE   The United Grand Lodge of England

Acknowledgements

I would like to thank a number of people for their help during my research for this book; first and foremost Dave Taylor and David Hughes for their assistance in giving me access to the York Grand Lodge documents, rolls and minute books, along with the artefacts of the York Grand Lodge. Thanks are also given to Martin Cherry from the Library and Archives of the UGLE, Paul Booth for help in transcribing certain documents, Keith Hatton from Jerusalem Preceptory No. 5 for giving access to their early records, and Richard Franklin from Arima Publishing for his continued support. I would also like to mention York Masonic historian Neville Barker Cryer whose valuable research continues to inspire. All photographs by David Harrison unless otherwise stated.

Foreword

David Harrison's newest work on the York Grand Lodge adds another significant chapter in his series of books on Freemasonry in England during the 18th and 19 centuries. One of the great strengths of his research is that understanding the social and political context of organizations is an essential part of the story. His previous works clearly demonstrated that thesis, and this new book carries this forward in telling the fascinating story of the York Grand Lodge. His access to primary sources has enabled him to show that the rivalry of the York Grand Lodge was more than just competition with the Premier Grand Lodge at London. Its existence was intertwined with the last great political struggle of the Stuart monarchy to regain the throne of England and Scotland, and as such the explanation of the eventual demise of its early phase is as much explained by the defeat of the Stuart cause at the Battle of Culloden in 1745 as it is by internal Masonic events.

Masonic historians often tell the story of Freemasonry as if it were divorced from the history around it. Thankfully, there are historians such as Dr Harrison who understand the fallacy of that approach to the writing of history. His commitment to the canons of academic research means that his books are always anchored in the larger world of historical reality. You will find some surprises in this book, as well as some thoughtful lines of further inquiry and study.

The York Grand Lodge has always held a special place in Masonic lore, with the attachment of its name to one of the two major rites of Freemasonry in the United States. Now readers will know the true story behind this famous Grand Lodge, and how it almost successfully challenged the place of the two other Grand Lodges in England in the 18th century – the Moderns and the Antients – to a third place in the annals of Masonry.

John L. Cooper III, Ph.D.
Grand Master of Masons in California
May 1, 2014

Introduction

The York Grand Lodge has a fascinating history; one that dates back to the early eighteenth century and, if one was to look at the practice of 'speculative' Freemasonry in Yorkshire as a whole, it can be traced to the later seventeenth century at least. I have written about the York Grand Lodge briefly in my first book *The Genesis of Freemasonry*, putting forward that it was a staunchly independent Grand Lodge, and especially in its later revival, one that was viewed as rebellious and schismatic. In short, the York Grand Lodge reacted against the claims of superiority by the 'Premier' or 'Modern' Grand Lodge of England in London. Indeed, in this book, which I envisioned as a companion book to my recent work on the *Liverpool Masonic Rebellion and the Wigan Grand Lodge*, I will be examining this staunchly independent stance against the London Grand Lodge by York, and how the two Grand Lodges came into conflict; a conflict which prevailed throughout the eighteenth century and ultimately led to the demise of the York Grand Lodge.

Rebellion is indeed a theme of this book; the York Grand Lodge having had a number of Jacobite supporters within their ranks, and it may have been this support that led to the Grand Lodge becoming dormant during the 1740s and 1750s, with the Jacobite rebellion occurring in 1745 and the retributions that occurred in its aftermath. The Jacobite rebellion was led by Bonnie Prince Charlie who attempted to regain the British throne for the exiled House of Stuart. The Jacobites were defeated the following year, but repercussions were harsh; not only for the surviving Highlanders involved but for Jacobite supporters in both Scotland and England.[1] The view that the rebellion affected the Grand Lodge has certainly been supported by Masonic historians such as Neville Barker Cryer,[2] though when referring to this period, the leading nineteenth century Masonic scholar Robert Freke Gould in his *History of Freemasonry*, did not present a reason why the York Grand Lodge went into hibernation at this time.[3] The political and religious persuasions of the leading

---

[1] See Fitzroy Maclean, *Bonnie Prince Charlie*, (Edinburgh: Canongate, 1989).

[2] Neville Barker Cryer, *York Mysteries Revealed*, (Hersham: Barker Cryer, 2006), pp.267-8. Barker Cryer states '*As the threat of Jacobite attempts to regain the English throne increased the danger which this posed to the harmony and even continued existence of the York Grand Lodge was realized.*' He then comments on the political divisions created in York Masonry, putting forward that '*the situation created between the 1715 and 1745 revolts now seems to have been such that at least those who were involved in public affairs locally could not sustain the kind of fellowship which the maintenance of even their illustrious Lodge would require.*' Barker Cryer supports this assumption by the fact that the records and furniture of the Grand Lodge were kept by appropriate members in readiness of '*being returned when circumstances were more favourable.*'

[3] R.F. Gould, *History of Freemasonry*, Vol.II, (London: Thomas C. Jack, 1883), pp.413-414.

members of the York Grand Lodge will be re-examined, and the disappearance of the Grand Lodge during this period will be discussed.

I will also put forward that there was an ongoing tension between the York Grand Lodge and the Premier Grand Lodge in London, from the conception of the London based Grand Lodge in 1717; a growing rivalry that certainly instigated the gathering of York Masons to term themselves as the Grand Lodge of all England in 1726. Unlike that other northern English independent Grand Lodge - the Wigan Grand Lodge - which emerged later as an outright rebellion to the union of the 'Moderns' and 'Antients' in 1813, the York Grand Lodge had older roots to localised Freemasonry; roots that assisted in York's affirmation that they were the source of Masonry in England, being founded by the Saxon Prince Edwin in 926 AD. This claim, though with its basis shrouded in legend, became a constant anecdotal precedent which gave the '*Yorkites*' - or so they believed - total English authority in regards to Freemasonry.

The revival of the York Grand Lodge in 1761 will be discussed along with aspects of continuity after its supposed demise in 1792; indeed, the work will consider that some subordinate 'York' lodges survived past this date, and that one lodge in particular may have survived until at least 1802. Along with new evidence of the possible survival of the Grand Lodge into the opening years of the nineteenth century, the continued influence of further degrees under 'York' will also be examined. Attempts by the York Grand Lodge of expansion into Lancashire will be discussed, along with an analysis of some of the Brethren who travelled into the neighbouring county to spread the word, and those who embraced this independent form of Freemasonry, being fascinated by its rituals. The book will also discuss how the York Grand Lodge continued to inspire; its ritual - or a form of its ritual - being used by certain local lodges, in some cases up to the present day.

This mysterious York Working will also be examined; its progression during the eighteenth century, and how and when other further degrees came to be practiced, such as the Royal Arch and the Knights Templar. The continuity of the York Grand Lodge can be seen not only in its influence on certain 'Modern' and 'Antient' lodges in Yorkshire and Lancashire, but also, as we shall see, in the practice of those further degrees by certain Masons in those areas; the story of the Grand Lodge, and its place in early Masonic history being a fascinating and intriguing one. Equally fascinating are the individual stories of the leading Brethren involved; Brethren such as Dr Francis Drake, William Blanchard and John Hassall, three vitally important York stalwarts that each contributed greatly to this independent Grand Lodge. It is certainly a testament to these men that the York Grand Lodge still inspires Freemasons today and captivates the interest of Masonic historians worldwide.

Chapter 1
The Grand Lodge of All England Held at York

'...the Building of Solomon's Temple, a Building where God himself was the Architect, and which to all Masons is so very particular, that 'tis almost unpardonable to neglect it...that with the Repairs of it by Josiah, rebuilding by Zarubbabel and Herod, to the final Destruction by Titus Vespasian...'

Dr Francis Drake, 1726.[4]

'...the Grand Lodge of all England — if we except the transitory Grand Lodge formed in London — never exercised any influence beyond Yorkshire and Lancashire...'

R.F.Gould.[5]

'His Lordship says he abhorrs the Thoughts of Tyrany in any Set of Men, and Particularly Maceons, and, if he is satisfied that the Grand Lodge of England has behaved improperly to the Grand Lodge at York, he will oblige them to make proper Acknowledgments for it; and will use his utmost Endeavours to promote a Reconciliation between the two Lodges, when he goes to London.'

Josiah Beckwith, 1779.[6]

During the celebration of St John which was held at the Merchants' Adventures Hall in the ancient walled city of York on the 27th of December, 1726, Freemason Dr Francis Drake gave a stirring speech; a speech that was bold and defiant. It was during this speech that a new *Grand Lodge of all England held at York* came into being, the York Grand Lodge declaring itself not just independent from the London based 'Premier' Grand Lodge of England, but as an older entity entirely.[7] It had been exactly a year since they had used the title 'Grand Master' for the first time, but Drake's speech delivered not only a new title, but outlined its history. This was based on a tradition that began in 926 AD. In this year, Prince Edwin, brother of the Saxon King Athelstan, supposedly presided over a meeting of Masons in York, which was seen as the

---

[4] Anon., *The Antient Constitutions of the Free and Accepted Masons, with a speech deliver'd at the Grand Lodge at York*, (London: B. Creake, 1731), p.16.

[5] Gould, *History of Freemasonry*, Vol.II, p.431.

[6] Taken from a transcribed letter written by the Master of Druidical Lodge; Attorney Josiah Beckwith to the York Grand Lodge, dated the 23rd of October, 1779, regarding Beckwith's visit to the Earl of Effingham, approaching him with the matter of accepting the title of Grand Master of the York Grand Lodge. York Grand Lodge MS. No. 67, Duncombe Place, York. See Appendix II.

[7] See Gould, *History of Freemasonry*, Vol.II, p.411, in which Gould states that there is no earlier mention of the title 'Grand Lodge of All England' before Drake's speech in December 1726.

first Masonic assembly in England. However, Drake in his speech referred to the seventh century King Edwin of Northumbria as a Grand Master, placing the beginnings of Masonry in York even earlier.[8] The fact that York was a Roman City littered with the remains of ancient classical architecture would also influence 'York' Freemasons such as Drake, who drew inspiration from the ancient ruins for his work *Eboracum*. Other leading York Freemasons such as Francis Smyth and Josiah Beckwith, as we shall see, also took a keen interest in local archaeology.

York was well positioned in the centre of the West, North and East Ridings, all forming the massive county of Yorkshire. Bordered with Lancashire which lay to the west, these two large northern English counties are separated by the wild, rugged hilly moorlands of the Pennines; the simmering rivalry of the two northern counties somewhat reflected in the harsh, unforgiving windswept landscape of the borderlands. It was this haunting landscape which would inspire writers such as the Brontë's; Branwell Brontë being a Freemason in Hawarth, West Yorkshire.[9] To travel from York to London in the eighteenth century could take about a week by coach, and York had established itself as a cultural centre of the north, with elegant buildings, theatres, printing presses, and was the residence of artists, writers, natural philosophers and of course Freemasons.

York, like the Roman city of Chester, has a strong tradition of medieval Mystery Plays associated with the ancient city's trade guilds, and like Chester, York also has a number of early references to 'speculative' Freemasonry dating back to the late seventeenth century, featuring prominent local families, merchants and tradesmen. These local gentlemen and Freemen of the city joined lodges and celebrated Freemasonry, at least in a social context, alongside operative Freemasons; finding the lodges attractive and somewhat enigmatic, and perhaps being drawn by the ancient mysteries of Divine geometry and

[8] See Arthur Edward Waite, *New Encyclopaedia of Freemasonry*, Vol. I, (New York: Wings Books Edition, 1996), pp.217-18. There is no existing evidence for Prince Edwin's York Masonic Assembly, many Masonic historians, such as Waite, dismissing it as pure legend. The Anglo-Saxon scribe Bede does write of King Edwin of Northumbria being baptised at York Cathedral in 627 and the rebuilding which took place at this time. Indeed, it is this reference that may have influenced Dr Francis Drake when he presented a date *'about the Six Hundredth Year after Christ'* for Edwin as *'Grand Master'* in York, when he gave his famous speech in 1726. However, Waite did acknowledge that a Prince Edwin existed in relation to King Athelstan, dating to around the time of the early tenth century, as there was an Edwin who appeared as a witness to Athelstan's signature on an extant charter at Winchester. This later date for Edwin, presented as AD 926, was referred to in later writings of the York Grand Lodge, and can be seen for example on the York Grand Lodge board painted by Thomas Beckwith. The date of AD 926 as Prince Edwin's foundation of the Grand Lodge was also used by the 'Antients', and can be seen in the Warrant of the Lodge of Antiquity in Wigan. The Edwin legend was also used later by the Wigan Grand Lodge, and can be seen displayed in its minutes.

[9] Branwell Brontë, the lesser known brother of the Brontë sisters, was proposed and accepted into the Lodge of the Three Graces No. 408, Haworth, Yorkshire, on the 29th of February, 1836.

mathematics which had been used by the medieval operative Masons. Certainly many of the local gentlemen involved in the York Grand Lodge were interested in architecture, and as we will see, many of the early Presidents and Grand Masters had been on the Grand Tour and had been inspired by the classical architecture they had seen on their travels, rebuilding their estates with Palladian grandeur. During the medieval period, Gothic architectural splendour - as seen in York Minster and the many churches of the city - would also be a testament to the much revered medieval masons of York.

Medieval Masons in York

Christian activity at the site of the Minster dates back at least to Anglo-Saxon times; the chronicler Bede mentioning that King Edwin of the Northumbrians was baptized there in 627.[10] This was probably a wooden structure constructed on the site, but a stone building was completed later. The church itself was built on the site of the old Roman headquarters of the city, and after being damaged during William the Conqueror's 'Harrying of the North' in 1069, rebuilding occurred and, around 1230, construction began on a glorious Gothic structure that was only finally completed in 1472. The subsequent Reformation and Civil War took its toll on the Minster, and it was not until the nineteenth and twentieth centuries that extensive repair work was carried out.

Such extensive building work at York Minster during the medieval period demanded the long-term presence of operative stone masons, and indeed, there are records of such masons, such as Master Mason William de Hoton junior who was the draughtsman of the full size setting of an aisle window on the plaster floor of the York tracing house. William de Hoton junior had followed his father William de Hoton senior as a Master Mason, both working on the building of the Minster during the fourteenth century. Other Master Masons are listed throughout the Gothic rebuilding phase of the Minster, such as Thomas de Pakenham in the 1340s and William Hyndeley at the end of the fifteenth century. These all appear in the York Minster Fabric Rolls, the rolls revealing an account of the expenses paid during the building work at the Minster.

Certain rolls also give a unique insight into the hierarchal structure and the rules of the operative masons; such as when *'the principal and second masons, who are called their masters, and the carpenter...who have been received by the Chapter, and will be received in perpetuity, shall swear in the presence of the Chapter, that they shall perform the ancient customs written below by means of the other masons, carpenters and other workmen, and they shall be faithfully observed...'*[11] The masons would thus go to the Chapter and swear to observe rules to ensure punctuality, order and the finest

---

[10] John Marsden, *The Illustrated Bede*, (London: Macmillan, 1989), p.16.

[11] Taken from J. Raine, (ed.), Fabric Rolls of York Minster (1360-1639, with an Appendix, 1165-1704), Surtees Society, Vol. 35, (London: Mitchell and Son, 1859), pp.171-2. See also Barker Cryer, *York Mysteries*, p.82. Barker Cryer comments on the masons' lodge at York Minster and how it was used, presenting a brief translation of the Latin from the Rolls.

workmanship.[12] As early as the 1349, a mason's lodge is mentioned in relation to the building of the Minster; the lodge being a workshop where the masons could cut and dress the stone for use in constructing the building.[13] This lodge would also be a place where the masons could eat, drink and rest, and they could discuss and plan their work; in 1349 for example, the records of the Minster list the tools of the lodge; a '*magna kevell*' is recorded, along with '*mallietes*', '*chisielles*', a '*compas*' and '*tracyngbordes*'.[14] The use of aprons and gloves are also mentioned in the Rolls, with 'setters' John Taillor and John Bultflow being given money for two skins from which to make aprons and 18d. for ten pairs of gloves.[15]

Despite the completed structure of the Minster being consecrated in 1472, work continued for a number of years on the fabric, with Master Mason William Hyndeley for example designing a rood screen. Other building around York also demanded operative masons, such as the Bedern - part of the College of the Vicars Choral - which was completed in the fourteenth century, and of course the city walls, the castle and the many other medieval churches within York, all requiring both building and maintenance work by skilled stone masons.

It was within this culture of civic building in York that certain masons took on important roles in the service of their community, such as Robert Couper who was admitted a freeman in 1443 and was then appointed Chief Mason to the Corporation. He was also the leading mason in the building of the Guildhall. It is clear that masons were essential to the medieval development of York, and even when we reach the Tudor period, these craftsmen were still serving important offices for the community, such as carver Thomas Drawswerd, who became a freeman in 1496, Chamberlain in 1501, Sheriff in 1505, alderman in 1508, MP for York in 1512, and Lord Mayor in 1515 and also in 1523.[16]

Between 1558 and 1563, a group of English laws called the 'Statute of Artificers' was passed by the government of Elizabeth I, regulating the supply of labour, setting wages for certain classes of worker, and disallowing apprentices to look for work outside their parish, effectively restricting the free movement of workers. For the masons, this was particularly difficult, as they were restricted in travelling to other areas to repair and maintain Churches and other buildings. Other trades could still survive by serving their community; the Glovers, Brewers and the Smiths for example could ply their trade from a fixed

---

[12] Raine, p.171 and p.181.

[13] Ibid., p.17. See also Barker Cryer, *York Mysteries*, pp.82-3 and pp.125-6. See also D. Knoop and G.P. Jones, *Genesis of Freemasonry*, (Manchester: Manchester University Press, 1947), p.37. Knoop and Jones also discuss the lodge at York Minster based on Raine's work on the Fabric Rolls.

[14] Raine, p.17. Barker Cryer in his *York Mysteries*, incorrectly puts this year as 1399.

[15] Ibid., p.50.

[16] For a list of Sheriff's and Lord Mayor's of York see William Hargrove, *History and Description of the Ancient City of York, Vol. I*, (York: William Alexander, 1818), p.319-20. See also Raine, pp.91-2 and p.97. He is described as '*magistri Drawswerd*'.

location within the town or city, but those crafts relating to the specialist building trades who depended on travelling to other areas, were restricted. In effect, the powers held by the craft guilds were transferred to the English state.

The effects of the Reformation led nineteenth century Masonic historians, such as W.H. Rylands to comment that:

> '*The Reformation had a disastrous effect on the system upon which the guilds of Masons were based. The whole was changed. It is not surprising, therefore, to find that many of the operative lodges died out, and the members for the most part were probably scattered over the whole country. Some, however, as independent bodies, survived the storm, and lasted for a considerable period. Of course their use for ruling the trade generally of a district or town had largely, if not entirely, passed away. The speculative element lasted, and, in some instances at least, if they did not take entire possession of the lodge, they appear to have assisted in keeping it alive.*'[17]

The entries of masons as freemen in Chester for example seem to support this, with no masons appearing as freemen from the 1520s until the late 1650s. With the admission being based on whether their father was a freeman or apprenticeship, and with the cost of the privileges attached to the enfranchisement, the masons' absence from the Freemen Rolls during this 130 year period certainly reflects a downturn in demand for the trade in Chester, a downturn which would have affected the number of masons working in the area. Masonic historian Neville Barker Cryer in his work on York lodges during this period has also stated that there was an '*almost complete demise of the local building site lodges between 1530 and 1630*'.[18] Though in York during this period, despite a handful of masons who became freemen, including a small number who were listed as '*freemaysons*', the trade decayed, and as Barker Cryer stated in *York Mysteries Revealed*; '*the list of working masons began to diminish after 1540*', on the whole due to the fact that the religious centres such as the Abbeys and the chantry chapels closed.[19]

However, the stone masons' trade certainly seems to have recovered after the Civil War period as both in Chester and in York there were applications made by the masons for a new Charter for a stone masons' Guild. In both cases, the municipal authorities referred to the fact that there was already an existing body for the masons, however, the operative masons managed to put

---

[17] W.H. Rylands, 'Freemasonry in Lancashire & Cheshire in the 17th Century', *LCHS*, (1898), pp.131-202, on p.135-6.

[18] Neville Barker Cryer, 'The Grand Lodge of All England at York and its Practices', see <http://www.lodgehope337.org.uk/lectures/cryer%20S02.PDF> [accessed 21st of July, 2009]

[19] Barker Cryer, *York Mysteries*, pp.163-4 and pp.179-180. Barker Cryer refers to a relatively small list of seven men listed as either '*freemaysons*' or '*masons*', compiled by G.Y. Johnson that became freemen of York between 1619-1691. Barker Cryer suggested that by 1700, the non-operatives had used the new name of '*freemayson*' while the operatives had reverted to being called '*mason*'.

across a strong case that the existing masons Guilds were not adequate and, in York in 1673, and in Chester in 1691, the stone masons were authorised to combine with the Bricklayers and the Carpenters.[20] Similarly, in Canterbury, around 1680, the Joiners, Carpenters, Carvers, Masons and Bricklayers were all incorporated into one body.[21]

A similar occurrence can also be seen in London in 1677, when the Masons Company was formally incorporated by Royal Charter, which gave *'all and singular Masons Freemen of our said Citty of London or Westminster in the Suburbs of the same Citties or seaven Miles Compasse of the same on every side thereof by virtue of these psents shalbe one Body Incorporate and politick in deed and in name by the Name of Master Wardens Assistants and Community of the Art or Mistery of Masons of the Citty'.*[22] The masons certainly seemed to have recovered after the Civil War in Chester, York, in Lymm near Warrington, and especially in London, where the building of St. Paul's Cathedral under Sir Christopher Wren created a revival in the trade.[23]

Masonic historians Knoop and Jones in their work *The Genesis of Freemasonry* commented that it was *'likely...that* [the old York Lodge] *or some other lodge existed at York before 1705'.* In referring to a copy of the Old Charges called the Levander York MS, which dates to c. 1740, and is handwritten on the flyleaves of a copy of Anderson's 1738 edition of the *Constitutions*, signed at the end *'From York Lodge-copy'd from the Original...in the Year 1560'*, they point out that as the original is lost, it is unsafe to use as evidence of an existing lodge at that time. However, they ascertain that if the York Lodge existed in 1560, it would have been operative.[24] An examination of the evidence for early non-operative or speculative Freemasonry in York is now needed.

The Early References of Speculative Freemasonry at York
The earliest possible reference to non-operative or speculative Freemasons in Yorkshire was mentioned by Masonic historian Barker Cryer in his book *York Mysteries Revealed*, in which he identified two men who were named in an

---

[20] Barker Cryer, 'The Grand Lodge of All England at York and its Practices', see <http://www.lodgehope337.org.uk/lectures/cryer%20S02.PDF> [accessed 21st of July, 2009]. See also Neville Barker Cryer, 'The Restoration Lodge of Chester', a paper delivered to the November Conference of the Cornerstone Society, 2002.

[21] Rylands, 'Freemasonry in Lancashire & Cheshire in the 17th Century', *LCHS*, p.136.

[22] The original Charter of 1677 granted by Charles II was confiscated by James II, who replaced it with a Charter of his own in 1686. The Masons Company preferred the original Charter and an Exemplification of the original grant was obtained under the Privy Seal of Queen Anne in 1702, in which the whole text of the Charles II Charter was recited. A transcription of this Charter can be seen online: <http://www.masonslivery.co.uk/downloads/43073_Masons_Charter_Book.pdf> [accessed on the 15th of August, 2009]

[23] See David Harrison, 'The Lymm Freemasons; A New Insight into Transition-Era Freemasonry', in *Heredom*, Vol. 19, (Washington: Scottish Rite Research Society, 2011), pp.169-190.

[24] Knoop and Jones, *Genesis of Freemasonry*, pp.154-5.

introduction to a version of the 'Old Charges' written on a manuscript entitled the York MS No. 1, dated to c.1600. The introduction reads:

> *'An Anagraime upon the name of Masonrie*
> *William Kay to his friend Robt Preston*
> *Upon his Artt of Masonrie as Followeth:'*[25]

Barker Cryer put forward that the two men mentioned in the document were two local Freemen from York; William Kay who was accepted as a spurrier in 1569, and Robert Preston who was accepted as a fishmonger in 1571, suggesting that they were at least interested in and involved with '*Masonrie*'.[26] The manuscript is certainly a very important and intriguing document, especially when analysing the wording of the anagram which states '*Upon his Artt of Masonrie*', suggesting that the Robert Preston mentioned in the manuscript was certainly interested in the '*Artt*' in some form. Michael Baigent however, who wrote the rather sensationalist foreword to Barker Cryer's book, was less cautious and erroneously stated that these men had actually joined a lodge in York, when there is no actual mention of them being in a York based lodge at all.[27] These two men were connected with each other in some way to appear at the beginning of the document, but the precise nature of their involvement with '*Masonrie*' remains a mystery as there is no other supporting evidence; they were certainly involved in the writing of these 'Old Charges', perhaps in a similar way that the 'Old Charges' written for the lodge in Warrington mentioned by Elias Ashmole in 1646, was compiled by Edward Sankey, son of lodge member Richard Sankey.[28]

Moreover, the York MS No. 1, according to a written inscription on the reverse of the manuscript, was only presented to the York Grand Lodge in 1736 by Dr Francis Drake, stating it had been found during the demolition of Pontefract Castle, which occurred after its surrender as a Royalist stronghold at the end of the second stage of the Civil War in 1649.[29] Drake's grandfather,

---

[25] York MS No. 1, Duncombe Place, York. A photograph of this section of the parchment roll can be seen in this book.

[26] Barker Cryer, *York Mysteries Revealed*, pp.156-7.

[27] Ibid, p.vii.

[28] The version of the 'Old Charges' written by Edward Sankey are preserved in the British Museum, the document being known as the Sloane MS No. 3848, see W.J. Hughan, *The Old Charges of British Freemasons*, (London: Simpkin, Marshall & Co., 1872), p.8.

[29] For a further description of the York MS No. 1 see Hughan, *The Old Charges of British Freemasons*, pp.5-6. Hughan mentions that the document was presented to the York Grand Lodge by Drake in 1736, but Barker Cryer mentioned that the date was 1732; see Barker Cryer, *York Mysteries*, p.156. However, William Hargrove in his *History and Description of the Ancient City of York* gives the date as 1738, which is discussed in H. Poole and F.R. Worts, *"Yorkshire" Old Charges of Masons*, (York: Ben Johnson & Co. Ltd, 1935), p.110, where Poole and Worts suggest it could be 1736 or 1738. When York Lodge archivist David Taylor and I examined the written text on the reverse of

before being ordained as a vicar, was a Royalist officer and was present during the siege, so the manuscript could have been previously kept by Dr Francis Drake's family.[30] For much firmer evidence of non-operative Freemasonry in York, we have to look at the later seventeenth century.

Next, we have the evidence of a mahogany flat rule with a date of 1663, measuring 18 inches, now held by the York 'Union' Lodge, displaying Masonic symbols and mentioning three men associated with York:

Iohn Drake	William ✡ Baron: 1663
of Yorke	Iohn ✡ Baron

John Drake seems to have been collated to the Prebendal Stall of Donnington in the Cathedral Church of York in October 1663, and was a cousin of Dr Francis Drake's father; William Baron was made a Freeman grocer in 1662, serving as sheriff of York in 1677, and John Baron may have been a relative of his.[31] Again, no lodge is actually mentioned, but the evidence of the rule, the symbols, and the mention of a member of the Drake family and of a prominent Freeman of York is suggestive of a locally important gathering which certainly used the '*Artt of Masonrie*'. Thirty years later in 1693, a parchment roll entitled the York MS No. 4 - another copy of the 'Old Charges' - mentions six men who were members of a lodge in Yorkshire.[32] This version of the 'Old Charges' was written by a certain Mark Kypling, who, along with the other men named, have been associated with the Tees Valley in the North Riding.[33]

Though, as we have already seen, the York Grand Lodge only referred to itself as having a Grand Master in 1725 and as the actual 'Grand Lodge of all England' the following year, a shift which suggests a reaction against the London based 'Premier/Modern' Grand Lodge. Despite this, Gould in his *History of Freemasonry* suggested that it had its actual foundations much earlier, giving a date of 1705 in which a 'governing body' at York began. Indeed, the list of the 'Presidents' of this governing body begins in 1705, and as we shall see, their role was much like that of Grand Master. From 1712, we have the minutes

---

one of the four sheets of parchment that comprise the MS No. 1, the ink was faded somewhat, but we both agreed that the last digit looked like a six. If this is correct then the manuscript was given to the Grand Lodge as late as 1736, and was thus still very much in operation at that time.

[30] Hughan, *Old Charges of British Freemasons*, p.6. Hughan mentions that the grandfather of Dr Francis Drake wrote a *Diary of the Siege*.

[31] See Barker Cryer, *York Mysteries Revealed*, p.189. For a comprehensive list of the Sheriffs and Lord Mayors of York see Hargrove, *History and Description of the Ancient City of York, Vol. I*, p.327.

[32] York MS No. 4, Duncombe Place, York. For a description of the York MS No. 4 see also Hughan, *Old Charges of British Freemasons*, pp.15-16.

[33] Ibid. For the Tees Valley associations of the six men named in the York MS No. 4, see Barker Cryer, *York Mysteries*, p.191.

of this old Lodge at York displayed in a manuscript entitled the York MS No.7, which supplies positive evidence that lodge meetings were held intermittently throughout the year at various local Inns such as Luke Lowther's Star Inn in Stonegate and John Colling's White Swan in Petergate, both of the proprietors being members of the old York Lodge.[34] These lodge meetings were on the whole termed as 'private lodges', but were occasionally called 'General lodges' such as the one held at the house of James Boreham in Stonegate on St John's Day on the 24th of June, 1713, or at certain times during the Christmas period as 'St John's lodges', such as in 1716 and 1721.[35] By the time we come to the 27th of December, 1725, the term 'Grand Feast' is used for the first time after a procession to the Merchant's Hall.[36]

The following year, the York brethren began to regard themselves as an official 'Grand Lodge', claiming ancient superiority over the 'Premier/Modern' Grand Lodge of 1717, thus adding legitimacy to its status and producing the absolute title of the Grand Lodge of *all* England held at York.[37] Dr Francis Drake emphasised this point directly in his aforementioned speech at the Merchant Adventurers' Hall: *'...we can boast that the first Grand Lodge ever held in England, was held in this City; where Edwin, the first Christian King of the Northumbers, about the Six Hundredth Year after Christ, and laid the Foundation of our Cathedral, sat as Grand Master.'* Drake continued to highlight the rivalry with London, saying *'This is sufficient to make us dispute the Superiority with the Lodges at London: But as nought of that Kind ought to be amongst so amicable a Fraternity, we are content they enjoy the Title of Grand Master of England; but the Totius Angliae we claim as our undoubted Right'.*[38]

The response must have been ecstatic; Drake was claiming that the first Grand Lodge had met in York in the early seventh century, even earlier than James Anderson had put forward in the *Constitutions* of the Premier Grand Lodge in 1723, when Anderson had referred to Prince Edwin as Grand Master of a *'General Lodge'* of Masons at York, stating that Prince Edwin was King Athelstan's son.[39] Drake was thus not only disagreeing with Anderson's version

---

[34] York MS No. 7, displaying minutes of lodge meetings dating from the 19th of March, 1712 until the 4th of May, 1730, Duncombe Place, York. For a transcription of these minutes see Gould, *History of Freemasonry*, Vol.II, pp.271-4 and pp.401-4.

[35] Ibid. A St. John's Lodge meeting is also referred to on the 24th of June, 1729, the festival of John the Baptist.

[36] Ibid.

[37] Gould, *History of Freemasonry*, Vol.II, pp.407-8. Also see T.B. Whytehead, 'The Relics of the Grand Lodge at York', *AQC*, Vol.XIII, (1900), pp.93-5.

[38] Anon., *The Antient Constitutions of the Free and Accepted Masons, with a speech deliver'd at the Grand Lodge at York*, (London: B. Creake, 1731), pp.19-20.

[39] James Anderson, *The Constitutions of The Free-Masons*, (London: Senex, 1723), pp.32-3. See also Hughan, *Old Charges of British Freemasons*, p.20. Anderson also mentioned the tradition of a lodge meeting in York during the reign of Elizabeth I in the 1723 edition of the Constitutions. He added further to this in the 1738 edition, stating that the meeting in York took place on the 27th

of events in York; he was helping to establish a rival Grand Lodge with older traditions. The Edwin tradition – that of Prince Edwin of the tenth century being the '*son*' of Athelstan, and the assembly of Masons at York, had however, appeared in various versions of the 'Old Charges' since the mid-late sixteenth century, such as the Dowland MS – dated to c.1550, and of course the York MS No. 1.[40] The tradition was clearly still developing, as by the 1738 edition of Anderson's *Constitutions*, Edwin was mentioned as the brother of Athelstan, and not his son.[41]

Presidents and Grand Masters
York Masonry was controlled by a string of leading local gentlemen; a local elite which included the likes of Sir George Tempest Baronet, who is listed as being the first known 'President' in 1705, The Right Honourable Robert Benson, Lord Mayor of York (later Baron Bingley) who is also listed as being 'President' in 1707, and Admiral Robert Fairfax, who was MP in 1713 and Mayor in 1715, serving as Deputy President in 1721. These are just a few of the local elite controlling York Masonry in the early years; powerful local gentlemen who were also influential in wider political circles.

The majority of the gentlemen involved in the early 'Grand Lodge' served in local government as Alderman, Sheriff, Lord Mayor or as Members of Parliament for York and the surrounding area, such as Sir William Robinson who was 'President' in 1708 and became MP for York in 1713, William Milner, who also served as a Member for York, and Edward Thompson Esq., who actually served as MP during his time as Grand Master in 1729.[42] The York Grand Lodge later kept this traditional link to the powerful Freemen merchants and tradesmen of the City, for example a grocer named Seth Agar was made a Freeman in 1748, became Sheriff in 1760 and Grand Master of the revived York Grand Lodge in 1767. Indeed, in Drake's speech of 1726, given in the Merchant Adventurers' Hall, which was the regular meeting place for the York Merchants Company, he addressed his audience '*To You, my Brethren, the Working Masons...To You, that are of other Trades and Occupations, and have the Honour to be admitted into this Society...And now, Gentlemen, I have reserv'd my last Admonitions for You...*', again

---

of December, 1561, with Sir Thomas Sackville as Grand Master, making some of the men Freemasons who had been sent to check on the lodge by Elizabeth I. The mention however, has no supporting evidence, and has led Masonic historians such as G.Y. Johnson and W.J. Hughan to dismiss it. Drake did not mention this tradition in his speech of 1726.

[40] For an analysis and transcriptions of the Dowland MS and the York MS No. 1 see Hughan, *Old Charges of British Freemasons*, pp.25-30 and pp.36-40.

[41] James Anderson, *The New Book of Constitutions of the Antient and Honourable Fraternity of Free and Accepted Masons*, (London: Ward and Chandler, 1738), pp.63-4. See also Knoop and Jones, *Genesis of Freemasonry*, p.77.

[42] Gould, *History of Freemasonry*, Vol.II, pp.407-8, and Whytehead, 'Relics at York', *AQC*, Vol.XIII, pp.93-5.

indicating a social mixture of not only 'operative' and 'speculative' Freemasons, but tradesmen and gentlemen as well.[43]

There is a list of all the York Grand Masters which starts from December 1725, but before that, beginning in 1705, as we have seen, the Office was termed as President. The gentlemen who held the Office were, on the whole, drawn from the local gentry; important affluent gentlemen of some status who held political power, and many, such as Benson, Tempest, Robinson and Hawkesworth, built or rebuilt their manor houses, being influenced by Palladian architecture; the fashionable interests in classical building perhaps in part, attracting them to Freemasonry. The society was evidently well established and important enough to attract such men of power, all of whom had obvious leadership propensities. The political persuasions of some of the Presidents and Grand Masters can certainly be noted as Jacobite, such as Charles Fairfax, Dr Francis Drake and Sir Thomas Gascoigne. Here is the known list and description of the men who held that Office from 1705, a list that includes not only the leaders of the localised community, but men of influence and standing in England:

Presidents of the old Lodge at York

1705: Sir George Tempest of Tong was the earliest of the known 'Presidents'. He was born on the 22nd of May, 1672, and was baptized at the Belfrey Church at York. He undertook extensive rebuilding work in the village of Tong; he rebuilt Tong Hall in 1702, along with the church of St. James in 1727, and he built the village school in 1736. He was buried at Tong on the 11th of October, 1745.[44] He served as President again in 1706 and in 1713.

1707: Rt. Hon. Robert Benson 1st Lord Bingley was born c.1676 in Wakefield, and became MP for Thetford in Norfolk from 1702-1705, before becoming MP for York from 1705-1713. He became Commissioner for the Treasury in 1710, Chancellor of the Exchequer in 1711 and Ambassador to Spain in 1713. He was also a director of the South Seas Company from 1711-1715, his political persuasion being that of a moderate Tory. Benson had been influenced by classical architecture on the Grand Tour, particularly Palladio, and built Bramham House in 1698. He died in April 1731 and was buried in Westminster Abbey.[45]

---

[43] Anon., *The Antient Constitutions of the Free and Accepted Masons, with a speech deliver'd at the Grand Lodge at York*, (London: B. Creake, 1731), p.21-22. See also G.Y. Johnson, *The Merchant Adventurers' Hall and its Connection with Freemasonry*, (York).

[44] Joseph J. Howard, *Visitation of England and Wales Notes, Volume 2, 1897*, (Berwyn Heights, MD, USA: Heritage Books, 1997), p.26.

[45] G.E. Cokayne; with Vicary Gibbs, H.A. Doubleday, Geoffrey H. White, Duncan Warrand and Lord Howard de Walden, (ed.), *The Complete Peerage of England, Scotland, Ireland, Great Britain and the United Kingdom, Extant, Extinct or Dormant*, new ed., 13 volumes in 14 (1910-1959; reprint in 6

1708: Sir William Robinson 1st Baronet was born on the 19th of November, 1655, and like his fellow illustrious 'Presidents', acquired numerous offices; he was MP for Northallerton from 1689-1695, served as High Sheriff in 1689, was also MP for York from 1698-1722, became Baronet of Newby on the 13th of February, 1690, and Lord Mayor of York in 1700. He was considered a Whig by Lord Carmarthen, and resided at Newby Park, a Palladian manor house built in 1718 by Colen Campbell. He died on the 22nd of December, 1736.[46] He was President until 1710.

1711: Sir Walter Hawkesworth 2nd Baronet was born in 1683 and served as High Sheriff for Yorkshire in 1721. He made many alterations to Hawkesworth Hall and its gardens, situated in the village of Hawksworth. He served as President again from 1720-1724/5, and died in York in March 1735.

1714: Charles Fairfax Esq. has been referred to as the brother of Sir Robert Fairfax,[47] but he was not. However, he was a member of the powerful northern extended family. His Jacobite leanings and his time as President will be discussed later.

1724: Charles Bathurst Esq. was mentioned by York Masonic historian T.B. Whytehead as possibly being the father to the Charles Bathurst who was the first Grand Master the following year.

1725: Edward Bell Esq. is mentioned in particular by Masonic historian Gould as a President for this year. Gould refers to a Dr Bell of Hull who wrote *Stream of English Freemasonry*, Dr Bell suggesting that Edward Bell or William Scourfield Esquires were Presidents in 1725.[48] Not much is known of Edward Bell, but Scourfield is mentioned as being Treasurer at the Grand Feast of the 27th of December, 1725. However, on the 6th of July, 1726, he was charged with calling a '*Schismatical Lodge*' the previous month on the 24th of June and making Masons without the consent of the Grand Master, as a result of which he was declared '*to be disqualify'd from being a member of this Society*' and to be '*for ever banished from the same.*'

---

volumes, Gloucester: Alan Sutton Publishing, 2000), volume II, p.178. See also <http://www.thepeerage.com/e290.htm> [accessed 21st of June, 2012]

[46] L.G. Pine, *The New Extinct Peerage 1884-1971: Containing Extinct, Abeyant, Dormant and Suspended Peerages With Genealogies and Arms* (London: Heraldry Today, 1972), pp.231-232. See also <http://thepeerage.com/p24141.htm#i2414086> [accessed 21st of June, 2012] and <http://www.historyofparliamentonline.org/volume/1690-1715/member/robinson-sir-william-1655-1736> [accessed 21st of June, 2012]

[47] See R.F. Gould, *The Concise History of Freemasonry*, (Dover Publications: New York, 2007), p.123.

[48] Gould, *History of Freemasonry*, Vol. II, p.408-410.

The other Brethren involved were given a chance to admit their '*Error in being deluded, and making such submission as shall be judg'd Requisite by the Grand Master and Lodge at the next monthly Meeting...otherwise to be banish'd...and their names to be eras'd out of the Roll and Articles.*'[49] Scourfield was typical of the leaders of the community that appeared in the York Lodge; being a druggist, apothecary and chymist who took the Freedom of the city in 1724 and was appointed Chamberlain two years later. Of the other Brethren implicated, a number were involved in the building trades, and Barker Cryer discussed a view put forward by Masonic writer John Yarker that this may have been a reason why there was a breakaway by Scourfield; the incident having reference to a dissatisfaction of the operative element.[50] However, there is no supporting evidence for this, though it could hint at some form of disagreement at the way the York Lodge was undergoing transition during this time as it moved to become a Grand Lodge.

Deputy Presidents of note

George Bowes Esq., the Deputy President mentioned in the York Grand Lodge minutes for 1712-13 was not, as Barker Cryer states in his book *York Mysteries Revealed*, Sir George Bowes (21st August 1701 - 17th September 1760) the English Member of Parliament, coal proprietor and ancestor of the Queen Mother.[51] However, they both belonged to the same extended family.

Admiral Robert Fairfax was of an omnipresent family, '*admitted and sworn into the honourable Society and fraternity of Freemasons*' on the 7th of August, 1713, and was the Deputy President mentioned in the York minutes for December 1721. He was born in February 1665/6, the second son of William Fairfax of Steeton and Newton Kyme in Yorkshire, and the grandson of Sir William Fairfax. He was commissioned to Vice-Admiral of the Blue in January 1708, but the commission was cancelled and given to another officer who was favored over him for political reasons. Fairfax was subsequently made a Rear-Admiral and a Lord of the Admiralty, but he retired from the Navy in the October. He then entered politics and at a by-election in 1713 he was returned to Parliament for York, but lost his seat in the general election after the accession of George I. Fairfax had in the meantime been elected as Alderman of York, and was elected Lord Mayor in 1715. He died on the 17th of October, 1725.

---

[49] Ibid., pp.401-3 and p.410.

[50] Barker Cryer, *York Mysteries*, pp.230-2.

[51] Ibid., p.225.

Grand Masters

1725: Charles Bathurst Esq. was baptised on the 1st of October, 1702, and on joining the York 'Grand Lodge' in July 1725, he replaced his father, who died in 1724 (the Charles Bathurst who was listed as being President in 1724 was, according to York Masonic historian Whytehead, most probably his father), Bathurst jnr becoming the first to hold the 'Grand Master' title on the 27th of December, 1725. Bathurst resided at an elegant Georgian Townhouse at No. 86 Micklegate, and a clue to his father's probable membership is a symbol used within Freemasonry, placed prominently on the downspout of the house; the Bathurst family crest which included the image of a snake eating its own tail, otherwise known as the 'Ouroboros', representing eternity, a symbol which is still used in Freemasonry today. His initials and those of his wife, Frances, are also on the downspouts.[52] She was buried at St. Martin-cum-Gregory church across the road.

Micklegate was a prestigious location that attracted the affluent members of York society; it had been the Royal processional route into the city. In 1727, an image of Bathurst House was included on John Cossins' *New and Exact Plan of the City of York* and, in 1736; Dr Francis Drake commented that *'very good new houses'* occupied the route. Charles Bathurst jnr died unmarried and the house became occupied by Abstrupus Danby, a local lawyer.

1729: Edward Thompson Esq. M.P. was born in 1697; he became MP for York in 1722, serving in the Office until his death in 1742. He was employed as a Commissioner of the Land Revenue in Ireland, and produced a pamphlet justifying the introduction of a general excise. This somewhat unpopular action, along with the pomp with which he conducted his affairs in Office, attracted the biting satire of fellow Freemason Jonathan Swift in his *'Advice to the Freemen of the City of Dublin in the choice of a member to represent them in Parliament'* which was published in 1733, Swift commenting on Thompson in his usual sardonic style:

'There is an Englishman of no long standing among us, but in an employment of great trust, power, and profit. This excellent person did lately publish, at his own expense, a pamphlet printed in England by authority, to justify the bill for a general excise or inland duty, in order to introduce that blessed scheme among us. What a tender care must such an English patriot for Ireland have of our interest, if he should condescend to sit in our Parliament! I will bridle my indignation. However, methinks I long to see that mortal, who would with pleasure blow us all up at a blast: but he duly receives his thousand pounds a year; makes his progresses like a king; is received in pomp at every town and village where he travels, and shines in the English newspapers.'[53]

---

[52] See the photographs of the townhouse of Charles Bathurst and the symbolism on the downspout.

[53] Jonathan Swift, 'Advice to the Freemen of the City of Dublin in the choice of a member to represent them in Parliament' (1733), in Temple Scott, (ed.), *The Prose Works of Jonathan Swift*, Vol.VII, Historical and Political Tracts – Irish, (London: George Bell and Sons, 1905), pp.309-317.

Thompson appeared to enjoy the pomp and ceremony of Office, and would certainly have taken great pleasure when bestowed with his title of Grand Master of All England.

1733: John Johnson Esq. M.D., took over from Thompson. Johnson had served as Deputy Grand Master in December, 1725.

1734: John Marsden Esq. was the final Grand Master that was listed until the revival in 1761. Marsden had first served as Warden in August 1725, and then on the Lodge Committee along with John Johnson Esq. M.D., in June 1729. Curiously, Marsden had advertised a *'Course of Chymistry'* in the *York Courant* in November 1729, at his residence in Stonegate, an interest that resounds in the lives of other Freemasons at this time, such as that energetic exponent of Newtonian natural philosophy Dr John Theophilus Desaguliers.[54]

The Revived York Grand Lodge

1761-2: Dr Francis Drake will be discussed at length later on, suffice to say that he was obviously the spiritual leader of the revived York Grand Lodge in 1761, and having proved his loyalty to the *'Yorkites'* in his speech to the Merchant Adventurer's Hall in 1726, he was undoubtedly the leading architect of the revival, a revival which was to become clearly seen as a rebellion by the Grand Lodge in London as the 'Moderns' increasingly saw the *'Yorkites'* as schismatics. His Jacobite leanings seemed to be almost a requisite for the position of Grand Master as we shall see.

1763: John Sawrey Morritt was the wealthy son of Jacobite and Tory Bacon Morritt of Selby. John, who had past family ties with Drake, purchased Rokeby Park in 1769, and his son, John Bacon Sawrey Morritt was a close friend of writer and Freemason Sir Walter Scott, Scott writing the poem *Rokeby* - set during the English Civil War and clearly influenced by his friend's country estate.[55] John Bacon Sawrey Morritt was also a founder of the Travellers Club in 1819 and was elected a member of the Dilettanti Society.

1765-1766: John Palmes Esq. was descended from a staunch Yorkshire Catholic family, a family of ancient lineage with links to the Tudor dynasty and to the aforementioned Fairfax family. The family resided at Naburn Hall, and

---

For Swift's as a Freemason, see David Harrison, *The Genesis of Freemasonry*, (Hersham: Lewis Masonic, 2009), pp.165-8.

[54] See Bernadette Bensaude-Vincent and Isabelle Stengers, *A History of Chemistry*, (Cambridge MA: Harvard University Press, 1997), pp.59-60. See also Harrison, *Genesis of Freemasonry*, pp.127-8.

[55] See Walter Scott, *Rokeby*, (Edinburgh: John Ballantyne & Co., 1813). Scott was initiated, passed and raised in Lodge St. David No. 36, Edinburgh, on the 2nd of March, 1801.

both John and George Palmes had joined the York Grand Lodge soon after its revival. John's Catholicism and the lineage of the Palmes family would have been well known in the locality of York; John and George being fitting Grand Masters for the newly revived York Grand Lodge.[56]

1767: Seth Agar was Sheriff of York in 1760.[57] He joined York Masonry in 1761, and soon rose up the ranks; he became Deputy Grand Master in 1765 and two years later served as Grand Master. Seth can be seen frequently in the minutes of the York Grand Lodge, and his nephew Francis Agar was to join the York 'Union' Lodge in 1809.[58]

1768: George Palmes Esq. was the elder brother of the aforementioned John. George was the head of the Naburn estate until his death in 1774 when it passed to his younger brother John, who died in 1783.[59]

1771-2: Sir Thomas Gascoigne, 8th Baronet was born in Cambrai, France, on the 7th of March, 1745, and died in 1810. Gascoigne was typical of the rebellious Jacobite York Grand Masters; he was an avid supporter of the American War of Independence, and built a commemorative arch to the American victory on his estate at Parlington, influenced by the Arch to Constantine in Rome. Gascoigne was also a Catholic, but he was received into the Church of England and became a Member of Parliament for Thirsk, Malton and Arundel in the 1780s and 1790s. Despite this, he built St. Wilfred's Church near to his estate in Aberford, for the Catholics of the area.[60] He later married Mary, daughter of James Shuttleworth of Gawthorpe and the widow of Sir Charles Turner. His only son from this marriage, also called Thomas, died tragically while out hunting, just months before his own death.

1773: Charles Chaloner Esq. was not, as Barker Cryer states in his book *York Mysteries Revealed*, the son of Robert Chaloner Esq. of Bishop Auckland,[61] but was his younger brother. Robert was born in 1729 and married Dorothy, the daughter of Sir John Lister-Kaye 4th Bt., in 1763.[62] Charles Chaloner was

---

[56] John Burke, *A Genealogical and Heraldic History of the Commoners of Great Britain and Ireland*, Vol. I, (London: Henry Colburn, 1834), pp.611-613.

[57] See Hargrove, *History and Description of the Ancient City of York, Vol. I*, p.330.

[58] See Barker Cryer, *York Mysteries*, p.348 and Wood, *York Lodge*, p.124.

[59] Burke, *Genealogical and Heraldic History*, pp.611-613.

[60] <http://www.barwickinelmethistoricalsociety.com/7428.html> [accessed 28th of January, 2013]

[61] Barker Cryer, *York Mysteries*, p.349.

[62] See Burke, *Genealogical and Heraldic History*, p.286 and Melville Henry Massue Marquis of Ruvigny and Ranieval, *The Plantagenet Roll of the Blood Royal: The Mortimer-Percy Volume*, (Berwyn Heights, MD, USA: Heritage Books, 2013), pp.254-6. After the marriage of Robert Chaloner and his wife

baptized on the 17th of May, 1736, at Auckland St. Andrew in Durham, both Charles and Robert being sons of William Chaloner Esq.[63] Charles Chaloner, who was described as a wine merchant of York, was also mentioned in a number of documents alongside Robert Chaloner as a devisee in relation to their maternal grandfather John Hodgson in 1763, and they appeared together in various land lease documents up until 1771.[64] A number of children of Charles Chaloner were baptized at St. Mary Bishophill Junior, in York, during the 1760s.[65]

1774-5: Henry Stapleton Esq. was born in 1741, and became a Captain of the Yorkshire Militia. Having inherited Wighill Hall, he refurbished it and was later referred to in the *Chronicles of the Yorkshire Family of Stapleton* as '*too generous a fellow*', lending money to his fellow military officers and various friends, and racking up a rather huge wine bill in 1769.[66] He died in 1779 at the young age of 38, leaving an only daughter Martha, who married Captain Chetwynd, second son of the fourth Viscount Chetwynd, in 1783.[67] The Stapleton family had deep-rooted Catholic traditions; both the Wighill and Carlton branches of the family continuing to adhere to Catholicism well into the 17th century.[68]

1776-9: William Siddall was a woolen draper who was made a Freeman in 1758,[69] served as Sheriff of York in 1765, and became Lord Mayor in 1783. He became Lord Mayor again in 1793 but died while in office.[70] Siddall was, as a

---

Dorothy in 1763, the eldest son John, was baptized in 1765. The Plantagenet Roll of the Blood Royal, *Being A Complete Table of All the Descendants Now Living of Edward III, King of England*, first published in 1911, includes an interesting list of Yorkshire genealogies such as the Chaloner and Wolley families, their lineages being known in the locality, and thus making Charles Chaloner and Edward Wolley important as candidates for the Office of Grand Master.

[63] The baptism register of Auckland St. Andrew, Durham, records Charles, baptized 17th of May, 1736, father William Chaloner, (DCRO, Ref: EP/Au.SA 3, p.126, entry 5), and Robert, baptized 3rd of March, 1730, father William Chaloner, (DCRO, Ref: EP/Au.SA 3, p.83, entry 6).

[64] Miscellaneous Documents relating to Robert and Charles Chaloner, (DCRO, Ref: D/X 649/137-151).

[65] The baptism register of St. Mary Bishophill Junior, York, records Robert baptized 14th of January, 1763, father Charles Chaloner; Charles baptized 7th of May, 1764 and William baptized 4th of March, 1766, father Charles Chaloner, (Borthwick Institute for Archives, University of York, Ref: PR.Y/M.BpJ/3).

[66] H.E. Chetwynd-Stapylton, *Chronicles of the Yorkshire Family of Stapleton*, (London: Bradbury, Agnew & co., 1884), p.472.

[67] Ibid.

[68] Ibid., pp.461-2. Also see Hugh Aveling, *Northern Catholics: the Catholic recusants of the North Riding of Yorkshire, 1558-1790*, (London: Chapman, 1966).

[69] See Francis Collins (ed.), *Register of the Freemen of the City of York: 1559-1759, Vol. II*, Surtees Society, Vol. 102, (1900), pp.262-289.

[70] Hargrove, *History and Description of the Ancient City of York, Vol. I*, p.330-1.

respected leader of the community, well suited for being Grand Master, and he also served as a City Alderman and as Collector of Stamp-Duties for the East Riding of Yorkshire and the Town and County of Kingston-upon-Hull.

1780: Francis Smyth jnr Esq. F.A.S was born in 1737 and resided in Newbuilding, Kirkby Knowle, and, like Drake, was extremely interested in the antiquities of Yorkshire. He died in 1809.

1782: Robert Sinclair Esq. was a Barrister at Law and Recorder of York,[71] born in 1747 and died in 1829. He married Elizabeth Sotheron in 1811, of the Sotheron's of Darrington Hall in Yorkshire. Robert belonged to the Holyhill branch of the Sinclairs from Ireland, and Sinclair became wealthy and influential in Yorkshire, the York Grand Lodge still securing prominent local gentlemen as Grand Masters even at this late date.[72] He was also a member of the York based Good Humour Club, and as we shall see, continued to be involved in Freemasonry in the area despite the decline of the York Grand Lodge.

1790: Thomas Kilby was a brewer who served as Sheriff of York in 1779 and as Lord Mayor in 1784.[73] He had become a member of the York Grand Lodge in January 1780, and like William Siddall, was a respected leader of the local community.

1792: Edward Wolley was the last known Grand Master of the York Grand Lodge, but the fact that he was elected into the Office proves that the York Grand Lodge was still functioning at this time. He was born in 1755, the eldest son of the Rev. Godfrey Wolley MA of Fulford Grange. He was an aspiring local gentleman, Wolley being a York based Solicitor and served as Undersheriff of York. He purchased the manor of Potto in 1808, and changed his surname by Royal Licence in 1810 to that of Copley, on inheriting Nether Hall in Doncaster.[74] Edward Wolley Copley died in November 1813,[75] and like Robert Sinclair and the Rev. John Parker, visited the York 'Union' Lodge in the opening years of the nineteenth century. A portrait of Wolley is in the possession of the York 'Union' Lodge No. 236, and hangs in the Banqueting Room at Duncombe Place.

---

[71] Ibid., p.332-3. The office of Recorder was described by Hargrove as '*next in dignity to the sheriffs*' and he must be a barrister at law. His duties are as guardian of the privileges of the citizens, preserver of ancient records, to register all new acts and by-laws, and to be a justice of the peace.

[72] See Roland William Saint-Clair, *The Saint-Clairs of the Isles*, (Auckland: New Zealand: H. Brett, 1898), p.323. See also Thomas Sinclair, *The Sinclairs of England*, (London: Trübner and Co., 1887).

[73] Hargrove, *History and Description of the Ancient City of York, Vol. I*, p.331.

[74] London Gazette, 19th of May, 1810. See also Marquis of Ruvigny and Ranieval, *The Plantagenet Roll of the Blood Royal: The Mortimer-Percy Volume*, p.256-7.

[75] The Gentleman's Magazine, Vol. 114, London, 1813, p.627.

The Early Workings of Freemasonry in York

Freemasonry in York at this time was not like the Freemasonry of today; the ritual, ceremonies and the way lodges met, were different, and reflect a form of Freemasonry that was undergoing a transition. For example, in 1705, at Scarborough, a 'private lodge' seems to have met for the sole purpose of admitting six men into the Fraternity, and in a similar manner as in Warrington, Lancashire, in 1646, when Elias Ashmole and Henry Mainwaring were made Freemasons, a version of the 'Old Charges', (known as the *Scarborough MS*) was used in the ceremony of admission. This seems to suggest that a special Masonic lodge could be formed using a drafted copy of the 'Old Charges', for the special purpose of admitting local gentlemen, Freemen or relatives of members; a temporary lodge formed by local Freemasons, which would appear, then disappear again after the ceremony.[76]

This occurrence of a temporary 'one-off' lodge also took place on a larger scale in Bradford, in 1713, when Masons under York met there, admitting 18 gentlemen of the local area into Freemasonry. In 1721, a Masonic meeting was recorded at Leeds and again at Pontefract, where it was recorded that *'several neighbouring Gentlemen were admitted'*.[77] At this time, there were only two 'parts' or 'degrees' being practised; that of Entered Apprentice and that of Fellow-Craft, and large groups of men could be admitted all at once; the two 'degrees' or 'parts' of the ceremony being performed at the same lodge meeting.[78]

In Chester, as in York, the make-up of the early lodges was strikingly similar, with many of the local elite being involved in a society which also included local Freemen and operative masons. Randle Holme III was a Chester based herald painter and a leader of the local community, his father and grandfather had also been Freemen and herald painters, both serving as Mayor. Holme compiled a list of 26 members of a Chester lodge in 1673 (including himself), the list revealing a mix of local gentry and men of the building trades including six masons.[79] The men on the list who were involved in local politics included George Harvey (who was related to the prominent Chester Gamull family), Thomas Folkes and Richard Ratcliffe, and the lodge included a number of members who served as Alderman and Sheriff. The list also included ten members who became Freemen of the City, including the aforementioned Harvey, Folkes and Ratcliffe.[80] This early Chester lodge however, seems to be an example of an operative-speculative lodge in transition, with local Freemen

---

[76] See Harrison, *Genesis of Freemasonry*, p.36.

[77] Barker Cryer, *York Mysteries*, pp.225-6.

[78] See Harrison, *Genesis of Freemasonry*, p.112-120 and Barker Cryer, *York Mysteries*, pp.194-201.

[79] See Knoop and Jones, *Genesis of Freemasonry*, p.141 and p.151, where the authors put forward that *'most of the leading building-trade employers of the city* (Chester) *were members of the lodge.'*

[80] Holme's list transcribed in John Armstrong, *A History of Freemasonry in Cheshire*, (London: Kenning, 1901), pp.2-5. See also D. Knoop and G.P. Jones, *A Short History Of Freemasonry To 1730*, (Manchester: Manchester University Press, 1940), pp.68-9.

and prominent local men, such as Holme, being welcomed into a society that still included operative masons - a lodge not dissimilar to the one mentioned in Warrington by Ashmole and the Freemasonry that occurred in York.[81]

Unlike York however, Chester was said to have been one of the first provincial cities to come under the influence and jurisdiction of the newly formed Grand Lodge in London, and by 1725, lists are available of the members of three Chester lodges.[82] These lists contain names that are related to Freemasons mentioned in Holme's list of 1673, such as Thomas Foulkes, Thomas Gamull, and Alderman Edward Burrows, who were all from prominent Chester families; Burrows being related to Randle Holme through marriage.[83] Other local gentry families also feature in the lodge lists of 1725, the gentlemen having a large role in local politics, as well as holding prominent offices in the leading lodge in Chester, which met at the Sunn Inn in Bridge Street.[84]

The strong and close 'clique' of powerful local gentlemen seemed to rule the old York Lodge/Grand Lodge completely in the early decades of the eighteenth century. The Freemen tradesmen within the York Grand Lodge structure also had family connections within Freemasonry, such as Leonard Smith, who was also an operative mason. His son followed in his footsteps and also became an operative mason and a lodge member, revealing continued links between operative and the speculative Freemasonry in the ancient city. Another member; John Whitehead, a Freeman Haberdasher who became Chamberlain in 1700 and Sheriff in 1717,[85] was the great-great-great uncle of York Grand Lodge historian T.B. Whytehead.[86] Other members who had family connections within the York Grand Lodge included Dr Francis Drake, and it was not uncommon to see relatives serving alongside each other in the Grand Lodge, such as Thomas and Josiah Beckwith, Thomas and Robert Bewlay, Francis, John and Robert Consitt, and George and John Palmes.

Despite this seemingly harmonious image of close family ties within the old York Lodge/Grand Lodge structure, it is interesting that Charles Fairfax, who held Jacobite sympathies, was fined and subsequently imprisoned for recusancy in 1715. His house was searched and his gun confiscated, and he was eventually brought before Robert Fairfax (who was Mayor at the time), Sir Walter Hawksworth and Sir William Robbinson, all members of the old York Lodge. Another local gentleman present at Charles Fairfax's hearing was Sir Henry Goodricke, who married the daughter of another York Grand Lodge member,

---

[81] See Harrison, *Genesis of Freemasonry*, p.31. See also Harrison, 'The Lymm Freemasons', pp.169-190.

[82] Armstrong, *History of Freemasonry in Cheshire*, pp.2-5.

[83] Ibid.

[84] Ibid.

[85] Hargrove, *History and Description of the Ancient City of York*, Vol. I, p.328.

[86] Gould, *History of Freemasonry*, Vol.II, pp.407-8, and Whytehead, 'Relics at York', *AQC*, Vol.XIII, pp.93-5.

Tobias Jenkyns, who happened to be Mayor twice in 1701 and 1720. Jenkyns also served as MP for York in 1715, beating fellow candidate and old York Lodge member Sir William Robbinson.[87]

Dr Francis Drake also had Jacobite sympathies, though, as far as can be ascertained he did not become actively involved in any agitation. However, as we shall see in the following chapter, his friend and associate Dr John Burton became somewhat involved in Jacobite intrigues.[88] A later visitor to the York Grand Lodge who held Jacobite sympathies was local Catholic and Freemason William Arundell, famous for removing the skulls of executed Jacobites from the pinnacles of Micklegate Bar in York in 1754. Arundell spent time in gaol for his actions, though having visited the York Grand Lodge he was subsequently blackballed when he was proposed as a member.

In his all-important speech at the Merchant Adventurers' Hall in 1726, Drake commented that *'the whole Brotherhood may be called good Christians, Loyal Subjects, True Britons, as well as Free Masons',*[89] perhaps asserting that the York Brethren were as loyal as the staunch Hanoverian London based 'Premier/Modern' Brethren. The speech was widely circulated at the time, being published in London; though despite putting forward that the *'Yorkites'* were independent to the London Grand Lodge, Drake emphasised that, as Freemasons, they were still *Loyal Subjects*. In spite of this assertion, it is suspicious that the York Grand Lodge became dormant during the 1740s and 1750s, the period of the Jacobite uprising and subsequent reprisals.

The references to the York Grand Lodge become sparse as the 1730s progressed; there was a brief reference to the *'old Lodge at York'* in the 1738 edition of James Anderson's *Constitutions*, and in 1744, the first positive reference to the Royal Arch was made by a certain Dr Fifield Dassigny, writing of an assembly at York of *'Master Masons under the title of Royal Arch Masons'*. Gould, in his *History of Freemasonry*, suggested that this was an assembly under the Grand Lodge of All England held at York, and was the last recorded reference of the York Grand Lodge until its revival in 1761 led by Drake.[90]

Of all the local gentlemen involved in the York Grand Lodge, Drake was perhaps one of the most important. Drake was the son of a Yorkshire clergyman who had been the Vicar of Pontefract, and became involved in Freemasonry at an early age, being a passionate champion of the ancient traditions of the York Grand Lodge; zealously expressing the mythical links with Edwin's first Masonic assembly at York Minster.[91] He was critical of

---

[87] Ibid.

[88] Ibid.

[89] Anon., *The Antient Constitutions of the Free and Accepted Masons, with a speech deliver'd at the Grand Lodge at York*, (London: B. Creake, 1731), p.24.

[90] Gould, *History of Freemasonry*, Vol.II, pp.407-8.

[91] Anon., *The Antient Constitutions of the Free and Accepted Masons, with a speech deliver'd at the Grand Lodge at York*, p.24.

Desaguliers' and Anderson's changes to the Craft, and, like his southern
counterpart William Preston, Drake was a historian and promoter of the Art,
writing *Eboracum*; a groundbreaking history of York and celebration of its
architecture, which was published in 1736.

It was during this same year that Drake had presented to the York Grand
Lodge the Parchment Roll of Constitutions, which, according to the writing on
the back of the roll, had been found during the demolition of Pontefract Castle.
This certainly would have given Drake increased status within the close circle of
York Masons.[92] This important version of the 'Old Charges', now securely
dated to c.1600, could have been used to strengthen the York Grand Lodge's
claim of superiority over London.   Indeed, even in a mid nineteenth century
edition of Thomas Paine's *Origins of Freemasonry*, this document, along with other
versions of the 'Old Charges' in York's possession, may have been referred to in
the preface of the work, when the editor comments on the rebellions and
rivalries within Freemasonry:

> *'These two lodges* [London and Scotland] *soon began to quarrel about precedency; each
> endeavouring to prove its priority by existing records of labouring masons...established many
> centuries before. The Yorkites, it is believed produced the oldest documents.'*[93]

After the dormant period, Drake played a major role during the 'resurrection' of
the York Grand Lodge in 1761, serving as Grand Master until 1762.[94]   In the
next chapter, Drake's political persuasions and role as an antiquary will be
discussed further, along with other leading intellectuals, artists and natural
philosophers who were linked to the York Grand Lodge. As we shall see, the
forging of a cultural identity took place in York during the eighteenth century,
and certain members of the York Grand Lodge were at the forefront of the
intellectual scene that shaped that identity.

---

[92] This is the York MS No. 1, which has been dated c.1600, and is the same manuscript which has
the introduction mentioning William Kay and Robert Preston as previously discussed. See
Hughan, *Old Charges of British Freemasons*, pp.5-6. Hughan confidently uses the date of 1736 for
when Drake presented the manuscript to the York Grand Lodge.

[93] Thomas Paine, *Origins of Freemasonry*, taken from *The Works of Thomas Paine*, (New York: E.
Haskell, 1854), p.217.

[94] See Gould, *History of Freemasonry*, Vol.II, pp.407-8, and Whytehead, 'Relics at York', *AQC*,
Vol.XIII, pp.93-5.

Sir Walter Hawkesworth, President of the old York Lodge from 1711-1713 and again from 1720-1724/5. Only after 1725 did York have Grand Masters.

Admiral Robert Fairfax, Deputy President in 1721.

Dr Francis Drake, the first Grand Master of the revived York Grand Lodge in 1761.

Sir Thomas Gascoigne, Grand Master of York from 1771-1772. Gascoigne, a supporter of American Independence, was a Roman Catholic during his time in the Grand Lodge.

Robert Sinclair, Grand Master of York from 1782-1783. He became Recorder of York and later visited the 'Modern' York 'Union' Lodge in 1802.

Edward Wolley, the last known Grand Master of York in 1792.
Wolley also was to visit the 'Modern' York 'Union' Lodge in 1802.

Actor and theatre manager Tate Wilkinson, who became a Master Mason in the York Grand Lodge in 1771.

Chapter 2

Jacobites, Rebellion and Culture: Freemasonry in York during the Eighteenth Century

'The Speaker, skill'd in his profession, seizes instantly the Attention of his Hearers, and with a Secret Magic strikes upon the Senses...'

Bridge Frodsham.[95]

'For Garrick was a worshipper himself; He drew the liturgy, and fram'd the rites And solemn ceremonial of the day...'

William Cowper.[96]

'...for the evil and perverse inclination will extract malignity from a Howard, a Hanway, or a Mason.'

Tate Wilkinson, *Memoirs*, 1790.[97]

There were many intellectuals thriving in the dynamic cultural arena of Georgian York, and certain Freemasons of the York Grand Lodge were central to this scene; Dr Francis Drake for example was a Fellow of the Royal Society and wrote the first great history of York, *Eboracum* in 1736. His friend and associate Dr John Burton also published a history of the Church in Yorkshire entitled *Monasticon Eboracense* in 1758, and William Blanchard, the last Secretary of the York Grand Lodge was the proprietor of the York Chronicle from 1777-1836, also publishing some radical work during the period. Among York's scientific community was John Goodricke (1764-86), a gifted mathematician, chemist and astronomer, the Goodricke family having had connections to some members of the early York 'Grand Lodge'. Artists such as Thomas Beckwith, who joined the York Grand Lodge in 1777, was on hand to paint the York Grand Lodge Board, and renowned actors such as Bridge Frodsham and Tate Wilkinson became members, the localised Grand Lodge and its social sphere attracting some of the leading intellectuals, artists and strollers of the area.

York was also the location of some of the finest Georgian buildings in England; elegant townhouses such as Fairfax House, the neo-classical perfection of Burlington's Assembly Rooms, the Lord Mayor's Mansion House and the Theatre Royal. The cultured social scene of York had been attractive to the visiting Scottish nobility, and the York races became an important attraction, the

---

[95] Barker Cryer, *York Mysteries*, p.309.

[96] William Cowper, 'The Task', in John Aikin jnr, *Aikin's British Poets*, Vol. X, (London: Longman, Hurst, Rees, Orme & Brown, 1821), p.105.

[97] Tate Wilkinson, *Memoirs of His own Life*, (York: Wilson, Spence and Mawman, 1790), p.251.

ancient city having many fine Inns to accommodate visitors. Yorkshire had acted as a northern hotbed for Catholic sympathisers, with some of the leading gentry adhering to the old religion.[98] As we have seen, a number of influential York Grand Lodge members such as Drake, were openly Jacobite in their political outlook, an outlook that ultimately created an air of danger and uncertainty, especially during the rebellion of 1745. Despite this, York was a vibrant city of culture, a city that emanated the enlightenment of the eighteenth century, and this chapter will present an examination of some of the leading York intellectuals and artists; some who were York Freemasons and some who were merely connected to them.

Jacobites and Freemasonry

As previously discussed, the York Grand Lodge disappeared from the records completely during the mid 1740s, but it was not the only governing body of Freemasons in England to suffer during this period; the London Grand Lodge was also experiencing somewhat troubled times during the same time. The procession to the Grand Feast through London was discontinued in April 1745, and there was a slow-down in the creation of new lodges during the 1740s.[99] Even Horace Walpole commented on the downturn when, in 1743, he wrote '...*the Freemasons are in low repute now in England...I believe nothing but a persecution could bring them into vogue again.*'[100]

The Grand Lodge having been dominated by staunch Whigs such as Desaguliers and James Anderson, there were notable members who were Jacobites, such as the Duke of Wharton who had been Grand Master in 1722, and known Jacobites could enter the social nexus of the London lodges, such as Andrew Michael Ramsay, who had been a tutor to Bonnie Prince Charlie in Rome. Tories such as writer Jonathan Swift and critics of the Whig regime such as satirist William Hogarth and poet Alexander Pope could be part of London Freemasonry, reflecting how Freemasonry was a society that crossed the great political divide of early eighteenth century England.[101]

The Grand Lodge of Scotland also had members on both sides of the political divide; there were Scottish Freemasons who had links to the Jacobites, such as James, Earl of Wemyss who served as Grand Master of the Grand Lodge of Scotland in 1743 and whose son Lord Elcho took a leading part in the rebellion. The Earl of Cromarty, who had been Grand Master in 1737, also

---

[98] After the Dissolution of the Monasteries by Henry VIII, Catholics from Yorkshire took part in the Pilgrimage of Grace, an uprising against Henry's religious reforms, and Guy Fawkes, a Catholic who was involved in the failed Gunpowder Plot of 1605, was born and educated in York. Many leading Yorkshire families, such as the Palmes family, remained openly Catholic.

[99] See Harrison, *Genesis of Freemasonry*, pp.180-1.

[100] Horace Walpole, *The letters of Horace Walpole, Earl of Oxford: including numerous letters now first published from the original manuscripts*, (Philadelphia: Lea and Blanchard, 1842), pp.321-2.

[101] See Harrison, *Genesis of Freemasonry*, pp.162-172.

joined the rebellion, as did William Boyd, 4th Earl of Kilmarnock, who was Grand Master in 1742. Other notable Scottish Freemasons however were anti-Jacobite, such as George Drummond, Lord Provost of Edinburgh, who served as Grand Master in 1752 and Lord Boyd (the son of the aforementioned William Boyd) who served as Grand Master in 1751.[102]

In Wales, Sir Watkin Williams Wynn 3rd baronet was a leading Jacobite and had promised Charles support during the rebellion, but he wisely stayed away from the Jacobite forces as they advanced through England. Wynn was however linked to the secret Jacobite society The Circle of the White Rose, taking its name from the white rose of York. A short lived Masonic lodge was also founded at the family residence Wynnstay in 1771 by his son, the 4th baronet.[103] Interestingly, Jacobite Bacon Morritt, Treasurer of the County Hospital at York and close associate of Dr John Burton and Dr Francis Drake, was also said to have toasted the 'King over the water' over a rosewater bowl.[104]

Unlike the London and Scottish Grand Lodges, the York Grand Lodge went into hibernation during the 1740s and 1750s. York was completely bypassed by the Jacobite forces, which passed through Carlisle in Cumberland, Preston and Manchester in Lancashire, and finally reached Derby before retreating back into Scotland using the same route.[105] The leaders of the community of York pledged allegiance to George II, but as we have seen, Drake was, at this time, undoubtedly the most influential of the York Grand Lodge members, and was an open Jacobite. His outspoken Tory associate Dr John Burton was also drawn into Jacobite intrigues, which, as we shall see, led to a set of events that was displayed in public. Perhaps with an overall downturn in Masonry and the overt Jacobite links that Drake displayed, it was enough for the staunchly independent York Grand Lodge to lay low for a while; re-emerging in 1761, with Drake at the helm.

Dr Francis Drake, Lord Burlington and *Eboracum*

As we have seen in the previous chapter, Dr Francis Drake was an antiquary and surgeon, and was also the author of *Eboracum* - a groundbreaking work that dealt with the history of York, its title being inspired after the Roman name for the city. Drake was undoubtedly the spiritual driving force behind the rebirth of the York Grand Lodge in 1761, a rebirth that will be dealt with in the next chapter. Drake was born in Pontefract and baptized there on the 22nd of January, 1696. His father, also called Francis, was a Vicar in the town, and as we have seen, he had links through his family to York Masonry. As a child he was educated well

---

[102] Ibid., pp.173.

[103] Ibid., pp.173-4

[104] See Barker Cryer, *York Mysteries*, p.264. For an excellent analysis of the effect of the Jacobite rebellion in York see Jonathan Oates, *York and the Jacobite Rebellion of 1745*, (York: University of York, 2005).

[105] Maclean, *Bonnie Prince Charlie*, pp.117-131.

and learnt quickly, having a thirst for knowledge which continued throughout his life - something that perhaps assisted in the seemingly meteoric start to his career.

The young Drake was apprenticed to a York surgeon called Christopher Birbeck, who died in 1717 and, at the young age of 21, Drake took over the practice. Ten years later he was appointed to the prominent office of city surgeon of York, around the same time that he was becoming equally as prominent in the York Grand Lodge. However, despite his prestigious career and his role in the Grand Lodge, tragedy was to strike. Drake had married Mary Woodyeare in 1720 in York Minster; they had five sons, but only two survived childhood, and Mary herself died in 1728 at the young age of 35. The death of his wife may explain his obsession in putting together a new project; that of the history of York.

Drake was constantly seeking hidden knowledge and, beside his medical career, he balanced his work with his interests in antiquarianism, writing his monumental history of York. Drake had always held an interest in local history and was a somewhat keen researcher of historical manuscripts; indeed, the historical elements of his speech in 1726 and the parchment roll of the 'Old Charges' he presented to the York Grand Lodge in 1736, testifies to his interest in researching and collecting ancient local documents. In 1729, he contacted the leading Oxford based antiquarian Thomas Hearne asking for assistance in putting together a history of York, but nothing seems to have materialized from the request. However, with the aid of a number of other historians and collectors, including his brother-in-law the Rev. Thomas Barnard, the Master of the Free School at Leeds, he started work on his magnum opus. In April, 1731, Drake asked the city corporation for permission to inspect the ancient documents, which was granted; the corporation later granting him £50 towards the cost of printing illustrations for the work. Lord Burlington, to whom the book was dedicated, also played a role in supporting Drake during the time he spent putting the work together; having rescued him from an unjust imprisonment for debt while in London.

After a turbulent few years for Drake, the result; *Eboracum*, a somewhat hefty book of around 800 pages with the rather long subtitle of *The History and Antiquities of the City of York, from its Original to the Present Time; together with the History of the Cathedral Church and the Lives of the Archbishops of that See*, was finally published in 1736. There were 540 subscribers - a number of whom were members of the York Grand Lodge; good old Masonic networking providing some fine support. Elements of the work reflected the themes found in his speech to the Merchant Adventurers' Hall in 1726, with the importance of the history of York - architecturally and culturally - being strongly put forward throughout. Indeed, Drake confidently guaranteed his readers that '*There is no place out of London, so polite and elegant to live in as the City of York.*'[106] The work also criticized how London came into prominence under William the Conqueror, Drake writing how York was ravaged under the '*Tyrant*' who subjected his own people to '*the greatest slavery*'; the once superior Roman city becoming the second city of the kingdom - a theme that was certainly reflected in the treatment of the York Grand Lodge by its London rival.[107]

Lord Burlington was of course an ardent supporter of Drake and arguably deserved the dedication of *Eboracum*. Though no record exists of Burlington as a Freemason, he was listed in Anderson's *Constitutions* as '*displaying the Art*', and his circle, which included the architects William Kent and Colen Campbell, was responsible for numerous publications on the architectural designs of Palladio and Inigo Jones. Whether Burlington was, or was not, a Freemason, he certainly knew many, such as the poet, Alexander Pope, and architect, Nicholas Hawksmoor. He socialised with Grand Masters, such as the second Duke of Montagu, and discussed Roman architecture with later York Grand Master Drake, and perhaps as a non-Mason, Burlington could not discern between the London and York Freemasons. Even one of Burlington's draughtsmen, Samuel Savill, belonged to a lodge that met at the Cock and Bottle, in London's Little Britain.[108]

Burlington's Chiswick House in London has at least two rooms which clearly reflect Masonic symbolism; the Red and Blue Velvet Rooms. Both reveal an array of distinctive Masonic symbols and have their ceilings adorned with representations of the Heavens. The Blue Velvet Room, in particular, focuses on divine architecture, actually displaying 'architecture' as a goddess residing in the heavens, holding the compasses, accompanied by three cherubs, each holding Masonic tools. The goddess is also holding a plan of the Temple of Fortuna Virilis after Palladio, and is similar to Villalpando's reconstruction of the inner sanctum of the Temple; Burlington having his three-volume work in his library inventory. The room's measurements resonate Masonic influence, being 15 x 15 x 15 feet, a perfect cube, reflecting perfect architecture, and again having similar proportions to Villalpando's and Newton's versions of Solomon's Temple. The actual design of the Chiswick House was inspired by Palladio's

---

[106] Francis Drake, *Eboracum or The History and Antiquities of the City of York, from its Original to the Present Time; together with the History of the Cathedral Church and the Lives of the Archbishops of that See,* (London: William Bowyer, 1736), p.241.

[107] Ibid., pp.86-7. For a discussion on Drake's portrayal of William the Conqueror as a villain and how York was destroyed and struggled to rebuild its fortunes, see the excellent paper by Rosemary Sweet, 'History and Identity in Eighteenth-Century York: Francis Drake's *Eboracum* (1736)', in *Eighteenth-Century York: Culture, Space and Society,* (York: University of York, 2003), pp.14-23, on p.18.

[108] For the lodge at the Cock and Bottle, London, see John Lane's Masonic Records of England and Wales 1717-1894 online: <http://www.freemasonry.dept.shef.ac.uk/lane/> [accessed July 17 2007] and John Pine, *A List of Regular Lodges according to their Seniority & Constitution. Printed for & Sold by I. Pine, Engraver,* (London: Little Brittain end in Aldergate Street, 1735).

Villa Rotonda near Vicenza, the square plan and layout not only bearing a remarkable resemblance to Villalpando's plan of the inner sanctum of Solomon's Temple, but also representing a set of proportions, which fuelled Burlington's taste in classical architecture.[109]

Burlington had witnessed firsthand the classical architecture of Italy during his Grand Tour, and quickly became what was termed the *High Priest of Palladianism*. He had studied in depth the divine measurements as used by Palladio, incorporating meticulously the measurements used in Palladio's Rotonda, in his design of the villa. The Rotonda was Palladio's ideal villa, and best represents the relationship between Palladio and the Ancients. Here, Solomon's Temple was considered the ultimate source for the Greek and Roman orders, with Villalpando describing it as an embodiment of classical harmony that God had disclosed to Solomon. This harmony was thought to be the form of musical harmony, which both Pythagoras and Plato had discovered, a belief, which Villalpando disclosed in his writings.

Burlington also designed the Assembly Rooms at York, which had been based on the *Egyptian Hall* of Vitruvius, as interpreted by Palladio; the Rooms symbolising and celebrating the ancient classical Roman architecture of York.[110] Indeed, Drake celebrated the building in his *Eboracum*, stating that buildings of Roman York had actually been surpassed: '*The City of York possessed in the Assembly Rooms a structure that in all probability, the Roman Eboracum could never boast of and that it excelled Eboracum's praetorian palace where two Roman emperors resided and died and a third presumably was born.*'[111] Colen Campbell, Burlington's architectural cohort, also designed the grandest Palladian house of them all; Robert Walpole's Houghton Hall, which he began, in 1722. The Freemason, Alexander Pope, like Francis Drake, admired Burlington's good taste in architecture, and honoured him in his *Epistle to Burlington*, in 1731, the poet praising Burlington as a new Vitruvius:

> *"You too proceed! Make falling arts your care,*
> *Erect new wonders, and the old repair;*
> *Jones and Palladio to themselves restore,*
> *And be whate'er Vitruvius was before:*"[112]

---

[109] For more information on the possible Masonic influences on Chiswick House see Ricky Pound, 'Chiswick House - a Masonic Temple?', in Gillian Clegg (eds.), *Brentford & Chiswick Local History Journal*, Number 16, 2007, pp.4-7.

[110] See Philip J. Ayres, *Classical Culture and the Idea of Rome in Eighteenth-Century England*, (Cambridge: Cambridge University Press, 1997), p.111. Ayres discusses how Drake consulted Burlington during his research for Eboracum and how they shared an interest in the Roman architecture of York, Drake using Burlington's drawings for the Assembly Rooms (based on Palladio) in the work.

[111] Francis Drake, *Eboracum*, (York: Wilson and Spence, 1788), pp.240-1.

[112] Joseph Warton, *The Works of Alexander Pope*, Volume III, (London, 1822), p.289.

Drake was elected a Fellow of the Society of Antiquaries of London and, in 1736 he was also elected as a Fellow of the Royal Society. In 1741, he was appointed honorary surgeon to the new York County Hospital, retiring in 1756, although he was relieved of the position during 1745-6 because of his overt Jacobite sympathies; he refused to swear the required oath of allegiance to the Crown. The duties of this post were not time-consuming, and he continued to devote most of his time to historical work, though he did find time to publish a medical paper in the Philosophical Transactions in 1747/8. Between 1751 and 1760, he published, with the fellow Tory, bookseller and editor of the York Courant, Caesar Ward, the thirty volumes of *The Parliamentary or Constitutional History of England from the Earliest Times to the Restoration of King Charles II*, with a second edition, in twenty-four volumes, appearing in 1763. This was around the time of the revival of the York Grand Lodge, and it was also a time of creative revival for Drake.

By 1767 however, with Drake's health failing, he left York to live with his eldest son, Francis, who was the vicar of St Mary's Church in Beverley. He died there on the 16th of March, 1771, and was buried in the church, where a memorial tablet was placed by his son, William Drake. Despite his Office as Past Grand Master of the York Grand Lodge, there were no Masonic symbols or references on the memorial, and no mention of his burial in the York Grand Lodge minutes.[113]

Dr John Burton

Dr John Burton was born in Colchester on the 9th of June, 1710, the son of a London merchant. After graduating from Cambridge in 1733, he continued his training in Leyden, Paris, and Rheims, where he obtained the degree of MD. He returned to England, settling in Wakefield after marrying Mary Henson in York Minster, and finally moved to York in 1738. The inventor of obstetric forceps, Burton was immortalised as Dr Slop in Laurence Sterne's *Tristram Shandy*, considered by many to be the first modern novel. Sterne, an Irish-born clergyman who settled in and around York, had active connections with the Minster throughout his life; his uncle the Rev. Jacques Sterne, the Precentor at the Minster, being Burton's most ardent opponent, and thus he would have obviously been aware of Burton's medical career and blatant Tory political leanings. Burton, as we have seen, was an outspoken Tory; he was said to have actually met the Jacobite rebels near Settle during the 1745 rebellion and, on returning to York, he was imprisoned in the Castle gaol until March the following year, when he was sent to London to be placed under house arrest. It was here that he met Flora MacDonald, the young woman who aided Bonnie Prince Charlie to escape capture.[114]

---

[113] A memorial tablet to Drake can still be seen at St Mary's in Beverley.

[114] See Maclean, *Bonnie Prince Charlie*, pp.246-259.

Burton was a close friend of Drake, and it was his care for the poor and sick of York, which led to his scheme for the York County Hospital being founded in 1740, his friend Drake gaining his position there the following year. Despite being close to Drake and sharing the same Jacobite leanings, Burton was never a member of the York Grand Lodge, though his belief in the ethos of education and charity would have been recognised there. Despite the damaging Jacobite ties, Burton, like Drake, went on to publish a well-respected medical work; *An Essay towards a complete new system of Midwifery* in 1751,[115] and also like Drake, Burton had a passion for antiquarianism, publishing his *Monasticon Eboracense* in 1758. At least five of the 15 subscribers were York Grand Lodge Masons. Burton died in January 1771, and his monument is situated in the Holy Trinity Church at Micklegate.[116]

John Goodricke, Natural Philosophy and the Scientific Community of York
We have already discussed Dr Francis Drake who had a keen interest in classic architecture and became a Fellow of the Royal Society, but there was also another York based Fellow of the Royal Society who had a tenuous link with Freemasonry and the York Grand Lodge. John Goodricke was born on the 17th of September, 1764, and was educated at the highly influential and progressive Warrington Academy, an educational centre which had connections to a local lodge.[117]

Goodricke began observing the night sky through a friend's private astronomical observatory in York. He discovered and calibrated the variable brightness of stars, presenting his paper to the Royal Society aged only 19. He won the Godfrey Copley medal for the most significant discovery in science, an even more remarkable achievement considering he was profoundly deaf. The Goodricke family had also close connections with members of the York Grand Lodge; John Goodricke was a member of the Goodricke Baronet family of Ribston, Yorkshire, and Sir Henry Goodricke, had married the daughter of York Grand Lodge member Tobias Jenkyns, who served as Mayor twice in 1701 and 1720, and also served as MP for York in 1715.[118] Goodricke died on the 20th of April, 1786, of pneumonia, shortly after being elected as a Fellow of the Royal Society.

Thomas and Josiah Beckwith
As a cultural centre of the north of England, Georgian York was an attractive place to reside for artists and writers, and the Grand Lodge supplied a

---

[115] See P.M. Dunn, 'Dr John Burton (1710-1771) of York and his obstetric treatise', in *Arch Dis Child Fetal Neonatal*, 84, (2001), F74-f76, which presents a fine critique of Burton's essay on Midwifery.

[116] See the photograph of Burton's monument.

[117] David Harrison, *The Transformation of Freemasonry*, (Bury St Edmunds: Arima, 2009), pp.19-36.

[118] Whytehead, 'Relics at York', *AQC*, Vol.XIII, p.95.

networking nexus of wealthy gentlemen who sought talented artists for portraits and included an array of ancient mysteries to stir the creative passions. Artist and Arms painter Thomas Beckwith settled into the York Grand Lodge with ease; he was made an Entered Apprentice and Fellow Craft in the York Grand Lodge on the same day on the 31st of March, 1777. He was made a Master Mason later in the same year on the 24th of November, and was soon appointed Junior Grand Warden by 1778, and served as Senior Grand Warden for the year 1780. Thomas painted the York Grand Lodge Board which is now in possession of the York 'Union' Lodge No. 236, the lodge also having an engraving of his self portrait. Thomas was also a passionate local historian and genealogist; he collected pedigrees of Yorkshire gentry and compiled Arms and crests of families, a collection of which can now be found in the Yorkshire Archaeological Society.[119]

There were a number of Beckwiths who were members of the York Grand Lodge. It is hard to establish if they were all related, but as in the case with the York Grand Lodge, many members of localised extended families were involved throughout its existence. One such gentleman; Josiah Beckwith of Rotherham, has been referred to as the brother of Thomas by York Grand Lodge historians Whytehead and G.Y. Johnson.[120] Indeed, Josiah, who was an Attorney, was proposed by '*Bror Beckwith*' on the 8th of December, 1777, and after being made an Entered Apprentice and Fellow Craft on a meeting held on the 20th of March, 1778, '*Bror. Thos. Beckwith proposed Brors. Josiah Beckwith & Thos. Alderson to be Raisd to the degree of M.Ms*' on the 27th of April.[121] So Thomas did have a hand at proposing Josiah, and also worked with him for the petition for constituting a new lodge in Rotherham called the Druidical Lodge, the petition being presented at a York Grand Lodge meeting on the 12th of October, 1778.[122]

Josiah Beckwith was elected as a Fellow of the Society of Antiquaries in 1777, and in 1784 he published a revised edition of Blount's *Ancient Tenures & Jocular Customs of Manors*, which became a much celebrated work in Antiquarian circles. He also had an extensive library, which was sold after he became bankrupt. He had moved to London and died there in 1791.[123]

Strollers, the Punch Bowl Lodge and the Good Humour Club
The Punch Bowl Lodge – so named as it met in the Punch Bowl Tavern in York, was, as we shall see in the next chapter, originally a 'Modern' lodge that joined the revived York Grand Lodge in 1761. It only lasted a few years, eventually being abandoned as the newly resurrected York Grand Lodge became

---

[119] The Beckwith Manuscripts, Ref: MS60-79, Yorkshire Archaeological Society.

[120] See G.Y. Johnson, *The Subordinate Lodges Constituted by the York Grand Lodge*, (Margate: W. J. Parrett, 1942), p.44.

[121] Ibid.

[122] Ibid, p.45.

[123] Ibid., p.74.

more attractive to the comedians that predominantly made up the members of the lodge. Tate Wilkinson, who became a member of the York Grand Lodge in 1771,[124] was an actor and manager of the Yorkshire circuit theatres, operating in a variety of places such as York, Wakefield, Leeds, Hull and Doncaster. He was central to the thriving theatrical scene of Yorkshire during the latter half of the eighteenth century, and worked with some of the most notable and talented actors of the period outside of London. Bridge Frodsham, a leading member of the Punch Bowl Lodge, was perhaps the most renowned stroller being *'esteemed in York as a Garrick'*, and was said to have lectured Garrick himself about Shakespeare.[125] Tate knew Frodsham very well, and commented on him, and a number of his fellow actors from the Punch Bowl Lodge, in his work *The Wandering Patentee*.

The actors and comedians of the eighteenth century would certainly have been attracted to Freemasonry; the lodge room providing a perfect theatre for performing the ritual. Indeed, Frodsham's famous 'charge' which was subsequently published, gives an element of the dramatic rhetoric that he was renowned for, the language used providing a hint of how the Punch Bowl Lodge would have operated. The 'charge' also seemed to touch on the friction between 'Modern' and 'York' Masonry, putting forward that *'in the north, when I see it, notwithstanding the virulence of its foes, rising to its primeval state; it immediately occurs to me, that the institution came from Heaven itself...'*[126] The fact that York could attract such highly esteemed actors is certainly a testament to its cultural importance. The vital work done by Tate Wilkinson for the theatre in York can never be underestimated; in 1769 he paid £500 for a Royal Patent for the theatre, renaming it the Theatre Royal, and his company became renowned as the leading provincial company in England.

Bridge Frodsham was originally a member of Lodge No. 259, the 'Modern' Lodge which had begun to meet at the Punch Bowl, and when the lodge appeared on the 2nd of February, 1761, Frodsham was in the Chair. Other members of the lodge who were also attached to the York Company included William Leng, described by Tate Wilkinson as a ladies' man, earning him the nickname 'Beau Leng',[127] James Oram, James Granger and Samuel Crisp.

---

[124] York Grand Lodge minute book 1761-1774. Duncome Place, York. Wilkinson is listed as No. 95 in the list of members at the back of the book, being made a Fellow Craft on the 11th of February, 1771, and a Master Mason on the 8th of April of the same year. Barker Cryer puts forward that he may have been made a member by 1770, suggesting Wilkinson became an Entered Apprentice then; see Barker Cryer, *York Mysteries*, p.288. Wilkinson left the York Grand Lodge in 1775.

[125] See Sybil Rosenfeld, *Strolling Players and Drama in the Provinces 1660-1765*, (Cambridge: Cambridge University Press, 1939), pp.156-8.

[126] Extracts from Frodsham's 'charge' can be seen in Barker Cryer, *York Mysteries*, pp.307-9. Taken from the *Newcastle Free-masons Companion of 1777*.

[127] Tate Wilkinson, *The Wandering Patentee, Or A History of the Yorkshire Theatres From 1770 to the Present Time*, (York: Wilson, Spence and Mawman, 1795), p.48.

However, the lodge also attracted local gentlemen such as John and George Palmes, both of whom had earlier joined the revived York Grand Lodge, and local merchants such as Jonathan Tasker and Brother Ricard, who both became members in June 1761. Tasker and Ricard were also members of the Good Humour Club; a club that operated from c.1725-1800, which met at Sunton's Coffee House in Coney Street, York. The club merrily celebrated the twin virtues of companionship and conviviality - virtues that were not too dissimilar to the ones found in Freemasonry.

The club, which was also known as the Doctor's Club (each member was given the honorary title of Doctor), was one of the many gentlemen's clubs that operated in York during the eighteenth century, and included many local Freemasons throughout its life - both from the York Grand Lodge and lodges under the 'Moderns'.[128] Tasker was a silk mercer from Stonegate and became a Freeman in 1747, and was already a member of the York Grand Lodge when he joined the Punch Bowl Lodge, being Grand Treasurer and Grand Secretary, later serving as Deputy Grand Master. He eventually got into financial difficulties and in 1774, while acting as Grand Treasurer, the dire state of his affairs came to light and the Grand Lodge received a large sum from his estate to cover debts owed.[129] Other members of the Good Humour Club included Robert Sinclair who served as a later Grand Master for the York Grand Lodge, and Drake's old publishing cohort Caesar Ward. The club also later boasted a number of members from the 'Modern' Apollo Lodge, which had also met on Coney Street at the George Inn when the lodge was founded in 1773. Founders of the Apollo Lodge were ex-members of the York Grand Lodge, and its particular part in the York Grand Lodge story will be discussed at more length later.[130]

Gentlemen's Clubs and Societies were an integral part of eighteenth century English society, and along with Freemasonry, formed part of the thriving intellectual scene of towns and cities such as York. For example author of *Tristram Shandy*, Laurence Stern, was a member of the Demoniacks Club, which met at John Hall Stevenson's Skelton Castle in Yorkshire, renamed Crazy Castle.[131] Other leading societies included the York Agricultural Society, founded by the Scottish physician Dr Alexander Hunter FRS, who practised in York. These clubs provided a networking nexus for gentlemen; a brotherly

---

[128] See <http://goodhumour.laurencesternetrust.org.uk/history/members-of-the-club/> [accessed 22nd of August, 2013]. Two recently discovered minute books belonging to the Good Humour Club; a minute book dating from 1743, the other dating from 1781, led to research conducted by Hugh Murray for the Laurence Sterne Trust in 2013, and a subsequent exhibition regarding the history of the club was held at Shandy Hall during the summer of that year. See Appendix IV.

[129] See Barker Cryer, *York Mysteries*, p.332-3, taken from the York Grand Lodge minute book 1761-1774, September and December meetings, 1774. Duncombe Place, York.

[130] See Appendix IV.

[131] See Harrison, *Genesis of Freemasonry*, p.140 and p.173.

bond that supplied business contacts and a consortium of like-minded characters.

William Blanchard and the York Chronicle
William Blanchard appears on the list of Officers roll for York on the 9th of March, 1778, and was to become the last Grand Secretary of the York Grand Lodge.[132] He was also the proprietor of the York Chronicle for many years and printed many pamphlets; for the Grand Lodge itself,[133] and others that were quite outspoken and verging on the radical. Blanchard however, was not the first to publish the paper; in 1772 the York Chronicle was established as a rival to the York Courant, the only newspaper then published in the city. This new paper was published weekly by Christopher Etherington, bookseller and publisher, at his press in Coppergate, and the first number appeared on the 18th of December 1772 under the title of the York Chronicle and Weekly Advertiser. It was at first '*a quarto, containing four leaves*' and had a somewhat Tory interest.[134]

Etherington produced 3,000 copies of each of the first two numbers and distributed them free of charge; a price of 2½d. was fixed for the 1,650 copies of the third number. The circulation did not reach 2,500 until 1774, when the paper was renamed Etherington's York Chronicle; it was then a four-page folio. The circulation subsequently fell below 1,900 in May 1775, and decreased further as a result of an increase of ½d. on the price of the paper which followed the increased newspaper duty of 1776. With this increase in price, the paper was renamed Etherington's York Chronicle, or the Northern Flying Post and General Advertiser. The last number appeared on the 24th of January, 1777 following Etherington's bankruptcy.[135]

The paper continued to be published with the omission of Etherington's name from the title until, on the 21st of February, 1777, it was published by William Blanchard as the York Chronicle and General Advertiser. Blanchard made a great success of the paper, and it is no surprise that he was praised by the likes of William Hargrove, who described him as '*a very respectable native of the city*'.[136] Blanchard also printed numerous pamphlets and books, some being rather outspoken; such as *The Defence of Prisoners in York Castle for not paying Tithes*

---

[132] See the MS. Roll of the List of Officers of the Grand Lodge of All England 1761-1790, 9th of March, 1778. Duncombe Place, York.

[133] Blanchard published a sermon by the Grand Chaplain of York: John Parker, Vicar of St. Helen's York, *A sermon, preached in the parish-church of Rotherham, before the Most Worshipful Grand Master of the most ancient Grand Lodge of all England ... and the newly constituted Rotherham Druidical Lodge of Free and Accepted Masons, December 22, 1778*, (York: W. Blanchard and Co., 1779).

[134] A concise history of the York Chronicle is given in Hargrove, *History and Description of the Ancient City of York*, p.261. Arthur Edward Waite in his *Secret Tradition in Freemasonry*, p.51, stated that Blanchard had given '*all the books and papers*' of the York Grand Lodge to William Hargrove.

[135] 'Newspapers', A History of the County of York: the City of York (1961), pp.537-541. URL: <http://www.british-history.ac.uk/report.aspx?compid=36391> [accessed: 19th of May 2012]

[136] Hargrove, *History and Description of the Ancient City of York*, p.261.

against the Charges of George Markham, Vicar of Carlton, in Yorkshire, contained in his Book, entitled "Truth for the Seekers" in 1797, and The Prisoners' Defence supported, by the Authors of the Defence, which was printed the following year.[137] Besides serving as Grand Secretary for the York Grand Lodge, Blanchard was chosen as a member of the York Corporation in February 1790, and served as Sheriff in 1817.[138]

Blanchard looked after his nephew, also named William Blanchard, who became the famous comedian and actor, after the death of both the young William's father and mother. Despite being apprenticed by his uncle in the printing business, young William effectively ran off and joined a company of travelling comedians at Buxton; going on to perform in London where his talents were praised by none other than the writer and poet Leigh Hunt.[139] William Blanchard died in 1836, having managed the York Chronicle for almost sixty years as editor and proprietor. On his death, the paper was then published by Henry Bellerby as the York Chronicle and Northern Standard, until it was bought by the owners of the Yorkshire Gazette in 1839.[140] Blanchard became the last surviving member of the York Grand Lodge and was the custodian of their artifacts and minute books, more of which will be discussed later.

York was certainly a pulsating cultural centre during the eighteenth century, a centre that celebrated its unique heritage and one that began to forge a distinctive cultural identity of its own; in the arts, in its architectural splendour, in its politics and in its social scene.[141] It was a centre that emanated talented intellectual men; men such as Drake, and equally attracted them, such as Burlington. As historian Roy Porter put it in his excellent work *Enlightenment*, during the eighteenth century 'English men would set up a club where they could be at ease',[142] and this is most certainly true in York, though, as we shall see, in regards to Freemasonry, it had to be on their terms.

---

[137] See Joseph Smith, *A Descriptive Catalogue of Friends' Books, or Books written by the Members of the Society of Friends, commonly called Quakers*, (London: Joseph Smith, 1867), p.464.

[138] Charles Henry Timperley, *A Dictionary of Printers and Printing*, (London: Johnson, 1839), p.945.

[139] See Lawrence Huston Houtchens and Carolyn Washburn Houtchens, (ed.), *Leigh Hunt's Dramatic Criticisms, 1808-1831*, (New York: Octagon Books, 1977), p.326. William Blanchard was certainly a much celebrated actor of the period and a portrait of him as 'Sir Andrew Ague-Cheek of Twelfth Night' was mentioned in *The theatrical inquisitor, or, Monthly mirror, Volume 12*, (London: C. Chapple, 1818), p.145.

[140] 'Newspapers', *A History of the County of York: the City of York* (1961), pp.537-541. URL: <http://www.british-history.ac.uk/report.aspx?compid=36391> [accessed: 19th of May 2012]

[141] See Sweet, 'History and Identity in Eighteenth-Century York: Francis Drake's *Eboracum* (1736)', *Eighteenth-Century York: Culture, Space and Society*, pp.14-23.

[142] Roy Porter, *Enlightenment*, (London: Penguin, 2000), pp.440-1. Porter also comments on aspects of York's cultural and political life on p.40.

The Punch Bowl Tavern - location of the 'Modern' Lodge which joined the York Grand Lodge after its revival in 1761 and the French Prisoners of war Lodge that met there from 1762-1763.

The Red Lion at Rotherham, location for the Druidical Lodge which was founded in 1778.

The elegant Georgian townhouse of Charles Bathurst, Grand Master of York in 1725.

A study of the iron downspout of the townhouse of Charles Bathurst
revealing the Ouroboros.

The Merchant Adventurers' Hall, the location of Dr Francis Drake's famous speech
on the 27th of December, 1736.

York Minster - a medieval Gothic masterpiece. The Crypt was said to have been the location for the last meeting of the York Grand Lodge 'Royal Arch or Templar Encampment' on the 27th of May, 1778.

Bedern Hall, situated close to the Minster, and was the location of a convocation of the revived York Grand Lodge on the 12th of June, 2006.

A medieval stone masons' mark from York Minster in the style of a pentagram.

Chapter 3
The Revival of the York Grand Lodge[143]

'I find his Lordship has had Matters represented to him by the Grand Lodge of England, in their own Way, and looks upon us as Schismatics...'

Josiah Beckwith, 1779.[144]

'That diligent Antiquary has traced out to us those many Stupendous Works of the Antients, which were certainly, and, without doubt, infinitely Superior to the Moderns'

Dr Francis Drake, 1726.[145]

'I now inclose to You a Brief Account of the Grand Lodge at York with a Narrative of the Umasonick Conduct of the Nominal Grand Lodge (in London) *accompanied by a Manifesto. His Lordship very justly dislikes the Distinction of Ancient & Modern Masons. It is in Truth an Unmasonic Distinction and will be found an Inconsistent Term.'*

Drafted letter from York Grand Secretary John Browne to Josiah Beckwith, 1779.[146]

As we have seen, the lack of official York Masonic records during the 1740s and 1750s has led Masonic historians of the nineteenth century, such as Gould, to suggest that the York Grand Lodge went into decline. It has therefore been accepted that the York Grand Lodge became dormant during this period, but was hastily revived in 1761 when it became apparent that the 'Modern' Grand Lodge of London had spread its influence and invaded the territory of the old York Grand Lodge. The founding of a 'Modern' lodge by what was effectively a company of actors within the city walls at the Punch Bowl Tavern seemed to have triggered a reaction from a small group of original York Grand Lodge Masons, who quickly ejected the 'Modern' lodge, replacing it with their own lodge.[147]

---

[143] Part of this chapter has previously appeared in the article; David Harrison, 'The Last Years of the York Grand Lodge – Part One', in *The Journal of the Masonic Society*, the Masonic Society, Issue 23, (Winter, 2014), pp.16-23.

[144] Taken from a transcribed letter written by the Master of Druidical Lodge; Attorney Josiah Beckwith to the York Grand Lodge, dated the 23rd of October, 1779, regarding Beckwith's visit to the Earl of Effingham, approaching him with the matter of offering him the Office of Grand Master of York. York Grand Lodge MS. No. 67. Duncombe Place, York. See Appendix II.

[145] Anon., *The Antient Constitutions of the Free and Accepted Masons, with a speech deliver'd at the Grand Lodge at York*, (London: B. Creake, 1731), p.11.

[146] Johnson, *Subordinate Lodges*, p.56. See Appendix II.

[147] Gould, *History of Freemasonry*, Vol.II, pp.413-5, and Whytehead, 'Relics at York', *AQC*, Vol.XIII, pp.96-7.

The revival of the York Grand Lodge was the result of the involvement of six local gentlemen, led by Drake, and it soon began to flourish again, with nine lodges founded under its jurisdiction during the ensuing decades. Indeed, at the official 're-launching' of the York Grand Lodge, a number of brethren were present from the usurped 'Modern' lodge, some of whom actually joined the revived York Grand Lodge such as John Tasker and Malby Beckwith.[148] This revival and the events behind the 'hijacking' of the 'Modern' Punch Bowl lodge can best be seen in the official response to the 'Modern' Grand Lodge, which was proposed at a meeting in December, 1767, after a number of letters had been received from London, addressed to the Punch Bowl lodge:

'*That the Grand Secretary do inform the Grand Lodge in London that the Lodge heretofore held under their Constitution No.259...has been for some years discontinued and that the most antient Grand Lodge of All England held for time immemorial in this City is now the only Lodge held therein.*'

The letter then continues to state firmly that the York Grand Lodge is back in business, and has marked its territory:

'*That this Lodge acknowledges no Superior, that it pays homage to none, that it exists in its own right, that it grants Constitutions and Certificates in the same manner, as is done by the Grand Lodge in London...and that it distributes its own Charity according to the principles of Masons.*'

However, the letter ends with some politeness and respect for their fellow Masons under the Grand Lodge in London:

'*It is not doubted but the Grand Lodge in London will pay due respect thereto and to all Brethren praying Instructions or Relief by virtue thereof, as this Lodge has ever had a very great esteem for that in London and for all Brethren claiming privilege under it's (sic) authority...In any Thing that may tend to the general Good, or may concern the whole fraternity of Masons this Grand Lodge will readily concur with than in London, and will pay all proper respect to any Information that shall be communicated by it...*'[149]

The minutes of the Punch Bowl Lodge ended abruptly in January 1763; the lodge seemingly having come to a natural end, with the actors being absent for a number of months in the year due to their theatre work, the more prominent

---

[148] See the MS. Roll of the List of the Members names of that Revived the Antient Grand Lodge of All England in 1761and of all who has been made Masons therein since. Duncombe Place, York.

[149] See Barker Cryer, *York Mysteries*, p.327, taken from the York Grand Lodge minute book 1761-1774, the proposed letter to the Grand Lodge of London written in December 1767 by the Grand Secretary D. Lambert. Duncombe Place, York.

members such as John Palmes, Malby Beckwith and John Tasker became completely involved in the revived Grand Lodge.

The revived Grand Lodge soon re-established itself and seemed to continue where it left off; it began attracting the prominent men from the city and started to take part in civic activities, such as in 1767 when it was proposed that the Grand Master and members of the Grand Lodge should attend the laying of the first stone of a new bridge being built across the River Foss, the architect of which being none other than the Senior Grand Warden – Brother Joseph Atkinson.[150]   The following year, two prominent local gentlemen became members; Sir Walter Vavasour and Sir Thomas Gascoigne, and when Gascoigne was installed as Grand Master on the 27th of December, 1770, during the celebration of St. John, a procession of the Grand Lodge took place which included 120 Brethren accompanied by a band of music. To the sound of the ringing bells of St. Martin's in Coney Street, the procession left the York Tavern at 9 o'clock in the morning, and arrived at St. John's at Micklegate for a sermon, before returning back to dine at the York Tavern, after which, at 5 o'clock, the Grand Master was duly installed with the other Grand Officers. The style of regalia was defined; Grand Lodge Officers wore aprons of Mazarine blue, lined and bound, Stewards wore aprons of red silk, lined and bound, Master Masons wore aprons of white silk, lined and bound, and Fellow Crafts also wore white aprons, but not lined and bound.[151] This was a show of strength by a confident independent Grand Lodge; a Grand Lodge that was growing, and with that growth, came an interest in establishing more new lodges in their territory.

The majority of the new lodges that were to be founded by the revived Grand Lodge were located in Yorkshire, but an ambitious effort at expansion was conducted during the Grand Lodge's later phase; with a lodge and Knights Templar Royal Encampment being established in Lancashire, and a lodge being founded as far away as Macclesfield in Cheshire. The York Grand Lodge practiced five degrees by at least 1779; that of Entered Apprentice, Fellow Craft, Master Mason, Royal Arch and Knights Templar,[152] and this unique Masonic practice may have attracted Masons to lodges under York, aiding its expansion throughout the county and beyond.

Indeed, it is at local level where we can best examine how the York Grand Lodge actually worked and best discuss its legacy; its lodges working the York ritual, termed the York Working. Some lodges vanished without trace after a brief life, others, as we shall see, were replaced by either 'Modern' or 'Antient' lodges; these new lodges having a number of brethren from the pre-existing 'York' lodge, meeting in the same place, using the same furniture and in some cases, claimed to practice a variation of the York Working.

---

[150] York Grand Lodge minute book 1761-1774, 28th of September, 1767. Duncombe Place, York.

[151] Ibid., 27th of December, 1770. Also see Barker Cryer, *York Mysteries*, pp.329-331.

[152] Wood, *York Lodge*, pp.109-110.

Of course the York Grand Lodge had founded a lodge before; this early example being a **lodge at the Talbot Inn, Halifax**, which was constituted on the 22nd of May, 1738. This lodge however, did not last long at all; it first met on the 4th of July, but on the 1st of August, just less than a month later; the 'Modern' Lodge of Probity No. 61 was constituted, meeting at the Bull's Head in Halifax. Interestingly, one of the members of the York lodge; James Hamilton, was described as the landlord of the Bull's Head, so one could assume that the Lodge of Probity, the oldest surviving lodge in Yorkshire today, replaced the local York lodge outright, and one member at least continued his Freemasonry with the 'Moderns'.[153]

There are no membership lists available for the Lodge of Probity before 1762, but its first lodge history, written in 1888, discusses the conflict between the York Grand Lodge and the 'Modern' Grand Lodge during this time, quoting William Preston, who commented that the venturing into the West Riding of Yorkshire by the Grand Lodge in London '*was considered a third encroachment on the jurisdiction of the Grand Lodge in York, and so widened the original breach between the brethren in the north and the south of England, that from henceforward all further correspondence between the two Grand Lodges totally ceased.*' Despite this tension, there is evidence that the Lodge of Probity 're-initiated' members from the 'Antient' and possibly the York Grand Lodge as the eighteenth century progressed.[154]

The year following the revival of the York Grand Lodge saw the constitution of the **French Prisoners of war lodge at the Punch Bowl** on the 10th of June, 1762, for French brethren only. York was the residence of French prisoners during the Seven Years War; some were granted parole and allowed the liberty of walking a mile around the city. However, the lodge was soon to end, as by April the following year, the war was over, the prisoners left, and the lodge closed. The Punch Bowl Tavern however, is still going strong.[155]

A 'York' **lodge in Scarborough** had been recorded as early as 1705, and though this had been a special lodge to admit six men, a second lodge under York was mentioned meeting there on the 16th of August, 1762, at the Turk's Head. This 'revival' of a Scarborough lodge did not last long despite having established traditions in the coastal town, and seems to have come to an end around 1768. A letter sent to the Junior Grand Warden at York by a certain Thomas Hart in 1772 described what had happened to the lodge, bemoaning how the owner of the Turk's Head - William Jefferson - had the lodge jewels in his keeping, and would not surrender them until the York Grand Lodge had been consulted.

Apparently, according to Hart's letter, the lodge at Scarborough had been thriving but had sadly begun to wane; Jefferson had admitted two or three of his

---

[153] T.W. Hanson, *The Lodge of Probity No.61, 1738-1938*, (Halifax: The Lodge of Probity, 1938), pp.49-50.

[154] See Herbert Crossley, *The History of the Lodge of Probity No. 61*, (Hull: M.C. Peck & Son, 1888).

[155] See Barker Cryer, *York Mysteries*, pp.355-6.

friends '*who seem'd to prefer a large copious bowl of Punch to the inestimable mystery wch in time tired the most serious part of ye community so much that rather than have their purses deeply dipt into; that ye Lodge was forsook since which Jefferson has left the House & remov'd to a private one...*' It appeared that drinking had become the central part of the lodge evening, and the lodge closed as a result. The jewels and punch bowl finally found their way to a certain Mr Hall, whose widow passed them on to a Bro. Steel of the Scarborough lodge, who finally passed them back to the York Grand Lodge. The punch bowl however, is now missing.[156]

A **lodge at the Royal Oak at Ripon** was meeting by August 1769, and its Brethren took part in the Grand Lodge procession at York in December 1770 when Sir Thomas Gascoigne was installed as Grand Master. By 1776 however, William Askwith, the landlord of the Royal Oak and Worshipful Master of the Ripon Lodge visited the Apollo Lodge in York - a 'Modern' lodge - where he '*desired to be made a mason under the constitution of England in this lodge*', thus on the 22nd of June, in the same year, the Ripon lodge was replaced by a 'Modern' lodge which met at the same Inn; this new 'Modern' lodge having four members that had belonged to the previous 'York' lodge. This Royal Oak Lodge No. 495 lasted until 1828 when it was erased, but the De Grey and Ripon Lodge No. 837 which was constituted in October 1860, still survives and still claims to work some of the old York Working.[157]

On the 21st of November, 1769, a **lodge at the Crown Inn at Knaresborough** was constituted and, like the Ripon lodge, Brethren from the Knaresborough lodge attended the York Grand Lodge procession in December 1770 for the installation of Sir Thomas Gascoigne. Again, the landlord of the Inn where the lodge was to meet was involved; Robert Revell had been balloted and admitted in the May, and he was raised in the October with two other men; the Rev. Charles Kedar and William Bateson, all three being on the petition for the new Knaresborough lodge on the very same evening they became Master Masons. By January 1785 however, the 'Modern' Newtonian Lodge No. 499 had been constituted, meeting at the Elephant and Castle. Four of the petitioners for this new lodge had been members of the local 'York' lodge, and it seems that, like the Halifax and Ripon lodges, a number of the brethren had opted for the 'Moderns'.[158] The Newtonian Lodge was erased in December 1851.[159]

---

[156] Extracts from a Minute Book of the Lodge at Scarborough, which mentions six meetings in 1762 and one meeting in 1768, taken from a foolscap sheet held at Duncombe Place, York. Also see Barker Cryer, *York Mysteries*, pp.357-360.

[157] York Grand Lodge minute book 1761-1774, 31st of July, 1769. Duncombe Place, York. Also see Barker Cryer, *York Mysteries*, p.328.

[158] Barker Cryer, *York Mysteries*, pp.361-2.

[159] Lane's Masonic Records <http://freemasonry.dept.shef.ac.uk/lane/> [accessed 9th of June, 2012]

A petition for a lodge to be held at the sign of the **Duke of Devonshire Flying Childers** in Goose Lane, Macclesfield in Cheshire, was presented on the 24th of September, 1770.[160] This Cheshire lodge however, did not last too long, as an 'Antient' lodge was meeting at the same Inn four years later, wholly displacing the York lodge.[161] It seemed an ambitious attempt at establishing a lodge so far away from its administrative centre in York, but, as a Warrant was requested to set a lodge up there by a Brother Abraham Sampson, the York Grand Lodge responded positively and pro-actively; Sampson and the 'York' Brethren involved in setting up the new lodge had been barred from visiting an existing 'Antient' lodge in Macclesfield. It seemed during this period, with three Grand Lodges to choose from, disgruntled brethren could petition the rival bodies in the hope of starting a new rival lodge. The Macclesfield 'York' lodge disappeared and the 'Antient' Lodge No. 189 began meeting in the same Inn, being constituted on the 7th of June, 1774, removing to the Golden Lion twenty years later.[162] Sampson was next heard from trying to start a lodge in London, promising to send the 3 guineas still owed for the granting of the constitution for the Macclesfield lodge, and the a further 3 guineas for the London lodge. No money appears to have been sent, and nothing further was done.

In March 1773, a petition was made to form a **lodge at Hovingham**, and a certain Rev. Ralph Tunstall from the village became central to this lodge and was to be involved in a later lodge at Snainton after he had moved to nearby Malton. The Hovingham lodge seems to have disintegrated, and by 1776, it was no more.

However, a lodge to be held at the **New Inn at Snainton** was constituted at the end of 1778, though there is scant information concerning how long it actually existed. A toll gate had been erected at the small village of Snainton and the New Inn was opened in 1776 as a staging post to accommodate weary travellers on the main road from Malton to Scarborough. The man behind the petition was none other than the aforementioned Rev. Ralph Tunstall, who had been a member of the defunct Hovingham lodge, though this lodge seemed to follow the same fate.

The petition to form the **Druidical Lodge at Rotherham** was presented to the York Grand Lodge in October 1778, and it became quite a successful lodge; lasting at least into the mid 1790s - if not beyond. Its first meeting was followed by the Masons of the lodge and members of the York Grand Lodge walking in procession to the Rotherham parish church on the 22nd of December, 1778. This was an official celebration of the new lodge and a very public statement, as the Grand Master himself was present, and a sermon was delivered by the

---

[160] Armstrong, *History of Freemasonry in Cheshire*, p.309.

[161] Barker Cryer, *York Mysteries*, pp.362-3.

[162] Armstrong, *History of Freemasonry in Cheshire*, p.309.

Grand Chaplain the Rev. John Parker. The sermon was subsequently published by William Blanchard.[163]

John Hassall, a wine and spirit merchant, was a founding member of Druidical Lodge, and he will be discussed at length later, as his later adventures become important to spreading the influence of the York Grand Lodge further afield. Hassall was probably born in Chester and had originally been an Irish Mason, being a member of Lodge No. 375, which was based in Dublin. His fortunes took a downturn when he was imprisoned for debt at York Castle in 1780, Hassall writing a somewhat moving letter to the York Grand Lodge asking for help.[164] It appears that the Grand Lodge assisted Hassall, and after his release he moved to Manchester for ventures new. Another founding member of Druidical was Attorney Josiah Beckwith, who had the task of visiting the Earl of Effingham on behalf of the Grand Lodge, approaching him with the offer of becoming Grand Master in October 1779, an offer that the Earl turned down.[165]

The Druidical Lodge kept excellent records during their first few years, and during a meeting of the lodge on the 26th of March, 1779, an example of the antagonism between the York and Modern Grand Lodges was displayed when it discussed the situation of a Mr James Hamer who had been proposed as a member, but had since been admitted into the Rose and Crown Lodge No. 277 - a 'Modern' lodge in Sheffield. It was ordered that he should be *'for ever expelled'* from Druidical *'and excluded from this Society either as a Member or a Visiting Brother'*. However, when Hamer was passed in the Rose and Crown Lodge on the 14th of May, 1779, a certain Bro Joseph Antt of the York Grand Lodge actually visited the 'Modern' lodge.[166] Away from the watchful eyes of the York hierarchy, friendly interaction between Masons of the two Grand Lodges could take place.[167]

The Druidical Lodge met at the Red Lion Inn, and though York lodges appeared to have not been officially numbered, this lodge was later given the number of 109, perhaps as a further means of recognition in a country where all 'Modern' and 'Antient' lodges had numbers to distinguish them. Later in its life, the lodge developed a relationship with the 'Modern' North Nottinghamshire Lodge No. 587, which later reformed into the Phoenix Lodge;[168] the Tyler from

---

[163] John Parker, Vicar of St. Helen's York, *A sermon, preached in the parish-church of Rotherham, before the Most Worshipful Grand Master of the most ancient Grand Lodge of all England ... and the newly constituted Rotherham Druidical Lodge of Free and Accepted Masons, December 22, 1778*, (York: W. Blanchard and Co., 1779).

[164] See Appendix I for a transcription of Hassall's letter to the York Grand Lodge.

[165] See Appendix II for a transcription of Josiah Beckwith's letter to the York Grand Lodge.

[166] Johnson, *Subordinate Lodges*, p.50.

[167] The antagonism between the two Grand Lodges had reached a new height at this time, as seen in the letter from Josiah Beckwith to the York Grand Lodge. See Appendix II.

[168] The minute book of the North Nottinghamshire Lodge No. 587, which also includes in the latter half of the same book the minutes of the Phoenix Lodge, is kept at Duncombe Place, York. The North Nottinghamshire Lodge has minutes dating from the 30th of April, 1792 – 3rd of

Druidical bringing the jewels for the use of the constitution of the new lodge. However, the new 'Modern' lodge appears to have kept the jewels, and in June 1792, '*It was ordered, that the Secretary write a letter to the Druidical Lodge at Rotherham...to thank the Brothers for the loan of their jewels*'.[169] Three years after this, a certain Rev. Beaumont Broadbent who had originally joined Druidical, asked to be re-made and raised in the 'Modern' lodge. Interestingly the good Reverend was described in the minutes of North Nottinghamshire Lodge as '*being of the Antient Freemasonry*', and it was noted that he had '*requested to be made a Mason and raised to the third Degree according to our form...*'[170] A discount was also given to the Reverend in respect of his already being a Mason, as it was decided that he should '*be exempt from the fees for raising to the Second & Third Degrees.*'[171] The Brethren of North Nottinghamshire Lodge reformed as the Phoenix Lodge in Rotherham in July 1808, though four of its listed nine members had previously been in Druidical.[172] Additionally, the Phoenix Lodge now possessed the original 'York' Warrant and possibly some of their furniture, suggesting that the various surviving members of Druidical had merged with the 'Modern' lodge sometime earlier.[173] This lodge was only erased in 1838.

Arthur Edward Waite in his *Secret Tradition in Freemasonry* discussed how a certain Godfrey Higgins from Doncaster, sometime before 1836, went to York and '*applied to the only survivor of the Lodge who shewed me, from the documents which he possessed, that the Druidical Lodge, or Chapter of Royal Arch Masons, or Templar Encampment was held for the last time in the Crypt* [of the Cathedral at York] *on Sunday, May 27th, 1778.*' This last survivor of the York Grand Lodge was quoted by Waite as being Grand Secretary William Blanchard, and the gathering in the Crypt by the Royal Arch Brethren did take place. A Chapter at Rotherham was actually petitioned for in 1780, so the Druidical brethren could work the Royal Arch degree in their home town,[174] and a Royal Encampment of Knights Templar was also held in Rotherham so the Brethren could practice the fifth

---

February, 1808, the remaining Brethren then forming the Phoenix Lodge at Rotherham which has minutes dating from the 22nd July, 1808 – 30th of August 1819. According to John Lane's Masonic Records, the North Nottinghamshire Lodge was discontinued c.1803, and the Rotherham based Phoenix Lodge No.533 was consecrated in 1808, being finally erased in 1838.

[169] The minute book of the North Nottinghamshire Lodge No. 587, 22nd June, 1792, p.15. Duncombe Place. Not listed.

[170] Ibid., 10th of July, 1795, p.70.

[171] Ibid., pp.70-1.

[172] Ibid. The four Druidical Brethren mentioned in the list are James Wilkinson - WM, Matthew Dixon, Joseph Flint - Treasurer, and Joseph Medlam. The Rev. Broadbent had off course also joined North Nottinghamshire a number of years before.

[173] Ibid., the Inventory being made in July, 1808. For a transcribed version of the Inventory see Johnson, *Subordinate Lodges*, p.74-5. Johnson puts forward that as the Inventory contains so many items; the additional list consisted of the furniture '*taken over from the Druidical Lodge*'.

[174] See Arthur Edward Waite, *Secret Tradition in Freemasonry*, (Kessinger, 1997), p.50-51. See also Barker Cryer, *York Mysteries*, p.380.

degree. Druidical may have survived to 1795, the year Broadbent was re-made in the 'Modern' North Nottinghamshire lodge, but by 1808, the remnants of Druidical were to be found in the 'Modern' Phoenix Lodge, a fate which reflected some of the earlier 'York' lodges.

Despite the apparent success reflected in its expansion, the York Grand Lodge did experience some set-backs; in 1774, attendance at Grand Lodge meetings had dropped, but it steadily rose again to around 25-30 by 1778, probably due to the introduction of harsher punishments for non-attendance. This can be seen in a Grand Lodge meeting in May 1776, when the Grand Lodge ordered that Brother T. Bewlay had to pay all the arrears due from him if he did not attend the next Lodge night, his membership would be discontinued and he would be banned from visiting! The threat worked, and Brother Bewlay duly turned up at the next meeting, going on to serve as Junior Grand Warden.

The confidence of the Grand Lodge was certainly shaken when a 'Modern' lodge once again was founded in York itself, and to make matters worse, the lodge was founded by disgruntled York Grand Lodge members. The Apollo Lodge was founded in 1773, and became somewhat of a haven for various ex-members and prospective initiates who had been rejected by 'York'. For example, surgeon and ex-'*Yorkite*' William Spencer was a founding member and the first Worshipful Master of Apollo, another recognisable 'York' name was jeweller Malby Beckwith, who served as the new lodge Secretary, and merchants Richard Garland and Joseph Braint were also ex-'*Yorkites*'. Thomas Clifton was a 'York' reject who found a home at Apollo, being proposed as a member in November 1783.[175] There may have been a number of reasons why Spencer, Beckwith, Garland and the other members of Apollo who once belonged to 'York' had left; Spencer and Beckwith had previously been members of the Punch Bowl Lodge, but despite Spencer having risen to the dizzy heights of Deputy Grand Master of 'York', a 'Modern' lodge offered a wider networking system, and as there were restrictions on 'York' Brethren visiting 'Modern' lodges, leaving 'York' became the only option for some.[176]

Spencer became Deputy Provincial Grand Master of Yorkshire soon after Apollo was founded, and the lodge certainly sought prestige; with Provincial Grand Lodge Officers being routinely elected from Apollo. It also attracted high status visitors such as Provincial Grand Master Sir Thomas Tancred and the Grand Secretary James Heseltine. Ex-'*Yorkite*' Richard Garland followed Spencer as Deputy Provincial Grand Master in 1780, but he began to drift into debt and resigned his Provincial Office in 1786 and stopped attending Apollo the following year.[177] In 1788 he was accused by the Alfred Lodge in Wetherby

[175] Barker Cryer, *York Mysteries*, pp.426-9.

[176] Ibid.

[177] Ibid., p.461-462. Richard Garland was however still in contact with certain Brethren as he attended a Provincial meeting at the Merchant Adventurers' Hall in York on the 26th of August, 1789, which included a number of Brethren from Apollo as Principal Officers.

of not having passed money onto Grand Lodge that they had given to him. Scandal was averted when Apollo members reimbursed the money to the Alfred Lodge, but this seemed to mark a turning point for Apollo; money matters had been discussed previously by the lodge and Apollo entered a period of decline. Garland himself became bankrupt in 1795.[178]

As Apollo slowly declined, so did the Yorkshire Province, with Provincial Grand Secretary and Apollo member John Watson virtually working alone to keep the management of the Yorkshire Province running up until the opening years of the nineteenth century. Watson had written to the London based Grand Lodge in the February of 1802 stating that:

> '*The Lodge* [Apollo] *has not met for some years past. Our P.G.Master is so very infirm, as renders him unable to attend to the Duties of his Office, and the Lodge deserted. I was induced, in the hope of its revival, to take the whole weight upon my shoulders and have for some time back found it too heavy for me, as such, I was under the necessity of resigning.*'[179]

Watson however stayed in the Office for a few more years and was a regular visitor to the 'Modern' York 'Union' Lodge, with Watson sometimes being listed as '*of the Apollo Lodge*'. It was only in 1803 that the Lodge of Probity in Halifax corresponded with the York 'Union' Lodge in regards to 're-establishing' the Provincial Grand Lodge in Yorkshire.[180] By this time, as we shall see, the York Grand Lodge was in terminal decline itself, and the Apollo Lodge seems to have ceased working sometime around 1817, the same year that the large Yorkshire Province was divided in two.[181]

The York Grand Lodge did however go from strength to strength during the ensuing decades after its revival; it was founding new lodges, it still attracted leading local gentlemen such as Robert Sinclair and Edward Wolley, and they had even courted the Earl of Effingham as a potential Grand Master in 1779.[182]

---

[178] Ibid., pp.460-465.

[179] Ibid., p.463.

[180] Correspondence between the Lodge of Probity and the York 'Union' Lodge mentioned in the Minutes of the Union Lodge, York, No. 236, Book 10, 5th of September, 1803. Duncombe Place, York.

[181] There are no minute books for the Apollo Lodge after 1788, though there is evidence they continued to meet; Apollo member and ex-'*Yorkite*' Thomas Thackray became Deputy Provincial Grand Master after Garland, and Thackray seemed to hold the Office until his death in 1793, and John Watson - initiated into Apollo in 1783, served as Provincial Grand Treasurer, then as Provincial Grand Secretary, appearing as a frequent visitor to the York 'Union' Lodge (though never becoming a member) until his death in 1815. An example of Watson listed as '*Provincial Grand Secretary*' while visiting York 'Union', along with another visitor from Apollo, can be seen in the Minutes of the Union Lodge, York, No. 236, Book 10, 27th of August, 1802. Duncombe Place, York. The Apollo Lodge's number on the Grand Lodge roll was changed a number of times; its original number was No. 450, becoming No. 357 in 1780, and No. 358 in 1781. In 1792 it became No. 290, and after the union of 1813, it was given No. 368.

[182] See Appendix II.

The York Grand Lodge was also practising five degrees by the late 1770s, and their unique form of ritual coupled with their boasted ancient traditions certainly played a part in attracting the attention of various Masons to their style of working. One Mason in particular - William Preston - would cement the success of the York Grand Lodge at this time, by rebelling against the 'Modern' Grand Lodge and being a leading figure in a new rebel Grand Lodge which was proudly attached to York.

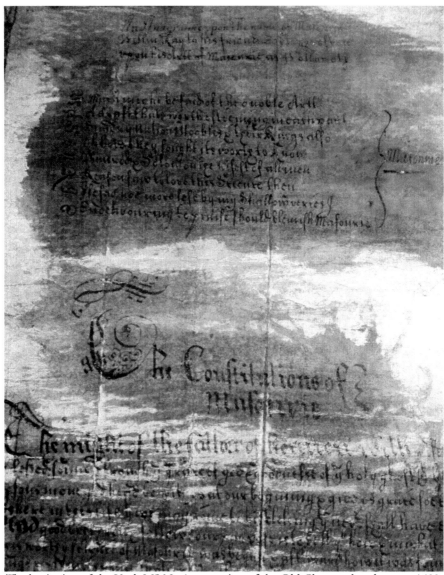

The beginning of the York MS No.1 - a version of the Old Charges that date to c.1600. They were presented to the York Grand Lodge by Dr Francis Drake in 1736.

The York Rolls, currently held by the York Lodge.

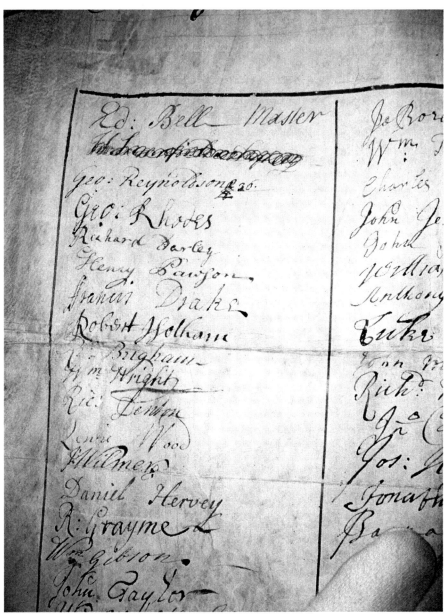

An early membership roll showing Edward Bell as 'Master'.
Francis Drake also appears further down the list.

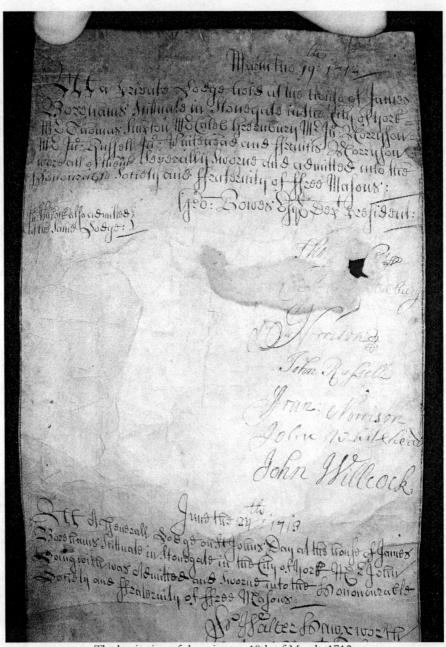

The beginning of the minutes: 19th of March, 1712.

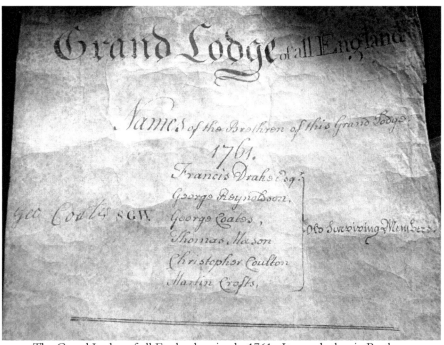

The Grand Lodge of all England revived - 1761. It reveals the six Brethren
- led by Drake - who resurrected the York Grand Lodge.

The York Grand Lodge Board, painted by Thomas Beckwith in 1778.

The memorial to Dr John Burton at Holy Trinity Church, Micklegate.
Burton was a Jacobite and associate of Dr Francis Drake.

Chapter 4
William Preston and the Grand Lodge of England South of the River Trent

'*Preston's version of the breach which occurred between the two Grand Lodges – London and York – is in the form of two distinct statements, one of which must be inaccurate, as both cannot be true. According to him, it arose out "of a few Brethren at York having, on some trivial occasion, seceded from their ancient Lodge, [and] applied to London for a Warrant of Constitution...to open a new Lodge in the city of York itself. This illegal extension of power...gave the highest offence to the Grand Lodge at York..."*'

R.F. Gould.[183]

'*But as to any Mediation with a Power acting so Arbitrarily as the Nominal Grand Lodge in London appear to have done We can by no means think of though as to any Individuals under their Sanction who will act on the Old Land Marks We will always pay due Attention to them agreeable to the true Spirit of Masonry.*'

Drafted letter from York Grand Secretary John Browne to Josiah Beckwith, 1779.[184]

'*...but departing from every Old Land Mark they exercised their Powers to form a new System and assumed an absolute Government watching unmasonlike to foment Divisions in the true Grand Lodge thereby attempting to crush the Head that rear'd em and having undermined their Way to the very ffountain they opend their own Channel just by it and set up a Constitution even in the City of York.*'

John Browne to Josiah Beckwith, 1779.[185]

This new rebellion within English Freemasonry led to the formation of yet another independent Grand Lodge called The Grand Lodge of England South of the River Trent, which was formed on 29th March, 1779. The Grand Lodge was however directly connected to the York Grand Lodge.

One of the leading figures behind this new Grand Lodge was the Masonic historian and writer William Preston. Ironically, Preston had written his *Illustrations of Masonry* a few years previously, which was to become a great influence on the Craft ritual of the future United Grand Lodge of England. The name of The Grand Lodge of England South of the River Trent, also echoes the

---

[183] Gould, *History of Freemasonry*, Vol.II, p.412.

[184] Johnson, *Subordinate Lodges*, p.57. See Appendix II.

[185] Ibid., this particular quotation comes from a 'crossed-through' paragraph in the Minute Book which is part of a draft letter from John Browne to Josiah Beckwith in regards to offering the Office of Grand Master to the Earl of Effingham.

desire for greater localised control, and can be seen as an 18th century statement on a north/south divide, as well as reflecting the schismatic theories on the Masonic ritual. The Grand Lodge of England South of the River Trent was short lived though, conforming in 1789 after an apology from all of the Brethren who had been expelled 10 years earlier was accepted by the 'Premier/Modern' Grand Lodge, with Preston and his colleagues becoming reconciled.

Preston was born in Edinburgh in 1742, first working as a printer, before moving to London where he entered journalism, becoming the editor of the *London Chronicle*. Soon after his arrival in London in 1762, he joined a lodge under the jurisdiction of the 'Antients'. This lodge had been formed by a number of Scottish Freemasons, coming from Edinburgh, who had originally planned to create a London lodge under the jurisdiction of the Grand Lodge of Scotland. However, the idea was rejected as it was thought the lodge may interfere with the 'Premier/Modern' Grand Lodge of England, so the Scottish Grand Lodge recommended the Scottish Masons to the 'Antient' Grand Lodge instead, who welcomed them.

In 1772, Preston instigated the transition of the lodge from the 'Antients' to the 'Moderns', and in the same year published his *Illustrations of Masonry*. He proceeded to deliver a series of lectures on Freemasonry, and joined the Lodge of Antiquity in 1774, where he instantly became Worshipful Master. Preston's illustrious Masonic career was both colourful and controversial; he reformed Masonic lectures and attempted to create a Grand Chapter in 1787, otherwise known as the Order of Harodim, which, despite its elaborate title, was merely a Lodge of Instruction, especially created to deliver his revised lectures on Masonic ritual. The Grand Chapter, which seems to have been controversial from the outset, died with its creator in 1818.[186]

Preston, perhaps attracted to the more ancient claims being made at the time, developed a liking for the York Grand Lodge, and in his *Illustrations of Masonry* he stressed the ancient origins of Freemasonry in York, and its subsequent influence all over Europe. He also suggested that there was antagonism between the 'Premier/Modern' Grand Lodge of London and the York Grand Lodge in the 1730s, which was a result of the increasing influence of the London based Grand Lodge within the territory of York. This claim is rejected by Gould in his *History of Freemasonry*, though Gould seems to be constantly critical of Preston, almost dismissing him as a mere maverick and continually siding with the 'Premier/Modern' Grand Lodge.

Having been a Freemason under the 'Antients', the 'Moderns' and the York Grand Lodges, Preston seemed to have been a figure who was constantly searching for something within Freemasonry, and was certainly interested in the historical and more mystical elements of the ritual. His frequent moves between

---

[186] Gould, *History of Freemasonry*, Vol.II, p.426. Also see Waite, *New Encyclopaedia of Freemasonry*, Vol.I, pp.292-3, and see William Preston, *Illustrations of Masonry*, (London: Whittaker, Treacher & co., 1829).

the various Grand Lodges, seems to reflect possible personal motives, for example, his move from the 'Antients' to the 'Moderns' in 1772, coincided exactly with the publication of his first major Masonic work, gaining instant prestige within the Craft. His Masonic career also attests to the fact that someone who was interested in Freemasonry at this time, had a choice of a number of Grand Lodges, all seemingly official, and all of which were competing against each other for prospective members.

Rebellion
The formation of the Grand Lodge of England South of the River Trent, erupted from a group of Freemasons from the Lodge of Antiquity, including William Preston, who decided to follow the Grand Lodge of all England held at York after a dispute within the lodge, which concerned an incident in which certain Brethren wore Masonic dress during a procession from the local Church to the lodge room. A small number of the Brethren took offence at this; Masonic public processions had been banned by the 'Premier/Modern' Grand Lodge since the early 1740s. They subsequently complained about Preston, who was then threatened with expulsion and forced to apologise.

Despite this, three of those who had complained were subsequently expelled by the majority of the Brethren at the Lodge of Antiquity. The lodge was ordered to reinstate the expelled Brethren by the 'Premier/Modern' Grand Lodge, but it did not, moving instead to join the York Grand Lodge.[187] The rebel Masons from the Lodge of Antiquity subsequently stole the lodge jewels and furniture, leaving a small minority from the same lodge to complain about their former Brethren, perhaps in a hope of distancing themselves from the rebels and to confirm beyond doubt their firm and unfaltering allegiance to the 'Premier/Modern' Grand Lodge.[188]

The rebels' approach to the York Grand Lodge is mentioned in the York minutes for August and September 1778; the York Grand Lodge asserted their ancient traditions and superiority in a reply to the Lodge of Antiquity in London, though they also wrote of their anger of a recently published 'Modern' Masons Almanack that had prophesised the rapid demise of the York Grand Lodge. However, defying the prophecy of impending doom with some glee, they agreed to grant the constitution requested by Preston. Antiquity duly answered by confirming that *'Should such a plan Succeed (we) shall be happy to spread the Art of FREE Masonry once more under the Banners of York and endeavour to convince the Gd. Lodge of London that the Prophecy of their Calendar Compilers is not likely to be fulfilled.'*

---

[187] Ibid.

[188] This action of the lodge splitting in two, with rebels defiantly forming a new Grand Lodge, stealing jewels and lodge furniture and leaving the loyal Masons complaining about their former Brethren, is mirrored in the future actions of some of the lodges that took part in the Liverpool Masonic Rebellion during the early 1820s. See David Harrison, *The Liverpool Masonic Rebellion and the Wigan Grand Lodge*, (Bury St Edmunds: Arima Publishing, 2012), p.48.

The York Grand Lodge agreed with Preston's 'plans' on the provision that York would be acknowledged annually and every constitution granted south of the Trent would be registered by York and the relevant dues paid.[189]

After joining the York Grand Lodge, the rebels were officially expelled by the 'Premier/Modern' Grand Lodge, creating a bitter feud that lasted for 10 years. They responded to the expulsion with the publication of a pamphlet written by the new rebel Grand Secretary Sealy, which protested against the '*disrespectful and injurous manner*" and "*the false, mean, and scandalous designations annexed to them*'.[190] The rebels then went forward to create a Constitution that turned their original Lodge of Antiquity into the Grand Lodge of England South of the River Trent, which was something of a coup for the York Grand Lodge - the Lodge of Antiquity being of course one of the four old lodges that had originally formed the 'Premier' Grand Lodge in 1717.

A copy of the 'Manifesto' issued by the new rebel Grand Lodge of England South of the River Trent was copied in the minute book of the York Grand Lodge after the December meetings in 1778. The 'Manifesto' stated the landmarks of Ancient Freemasonry as they recognised them, and asserted their right to withdraw allegiance from the 'Modern/Premier' Grand Lodge and place their lot with the York Grand Lodge, which they saw '*as the truly ancient and only regular governing Grand Lodge of Masons in England, to whom the fraternity all owe and are rightfully bound to pay allegiance.*'[191] The language used in the document did not pull any punches, and the document, which was to be published and sent to all known lodges, was obviously aimed at creating maximum impact - the document being a lexicon of Masonic freedom. Indeed, the 'Manifesto' produced by the Grand Lodge of England South of the River Trent is somewhat similar in form to the 'Manifesto' issued by the Liverpool Masonic Rebels in 1821; a piece of writing clearly inspired by this groundbreaking original.[192] The creation of the new rebel Grand Lodge certainly widened the rift between the York and 'Modern' Grand Lodges to seismic proportions, and later historians such as Gould were critical of Preston for his overt betrayal.[193]

This new Grand Lodge however, only had three lodges under its influence; the original being the Lodge of Antiquity, the second being the Lodge of Perseverance and Triumph which was constituted at the Queen's Head Tavern

---

[189] See Barker Cryer, *York Mysteries*, p.336-7.

[190] Gould, *History of Freemasonry*, Vol.II, p.426.

[191] See Barker Cryer, *York Mysteries*, p.338-9, taken from the York Grand Lodge minute book 1774-1780, written after December 1778. Duncombe Place, York.

[192] Harrison, *The Liverpool Masonic Rebellion and the Wigan Grand Lodge*, p.44. The 'Manifesto' drafted by the Liverpool Masonic Rebels in 1822 outlining their disgust at what they saw as the unjust treatment dealt to them by the UGLE. The printed document was then, like the one composed by the rebel Grand Lodge of England South of the River Trent, sent to all lodges under the Grand Lodge in London, to cause maximum effect and to gain support for their cause.

[193] Gould, *History of Freemasonry*, Vol.II, p.412.

in Holborn on 9th August, 1779, and the third being the Lodge of Perfect Observance, constituted a few months later at the Mitre Tavern in Fleet Street on 15th November, 1779. The early years of the Grand Lodge seemed to have gathered a popular following, but by 1789, a report to the Grand Lodge of all England held at York, commented that *'the decayed state of the two Lodges was taken into consideration'*.

After an investigation into the apparent grave situation of the Grand Lodge of England South of the River Trent, it was stated that *'upon the whole, the prospect before us seems to be less gloomy than that we have had for some time past'*. A statement, which seems to suggest that reconciliation, was being considered.[194] Preston died in 1818, and in his will, he left £500 to the Masonic Fund of Benevolence, and £300 to ensure the annual delivery of the Prestonian Lecture, which is dedicated to the study of the history of the Craft, and still continues today.[195] Despite criticisms from certain Victorian Masonic historians such as Gould, Preston's work did continue to influence future Freemasons, especially George Oliver, the 19th century Masonic historian who revised his *Illustrations of Masonry*.[196] And in the United States, Preston's version of the Craft ritual became immensely influential; the Preston-Webb ritual being used under most of the Grand Lodges there today.

---

[194] Ibid., p.427.

[195] Ibid., pp.421-8. Also see Whytehead, 'Relics at York', *AQC*, Vol.XIII, pp.112-5, which includes a transcribed *Copy of the Constitutions granted to the Lodge of Antiquity, creating them a Grand Lodge*, and other transcribed correspondence between the York Grand Lodge and the Lodge of Antiquity.

[196] R.S.E. Sandbach, *Priest and Freemason: The Life of George Oliver*, (Wellingborough: The Aquarian Press, 1988), p.34 and p.39.

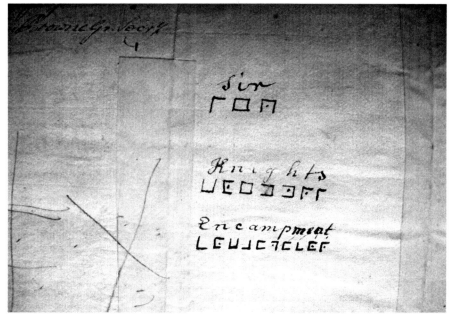

Knights Templar Cipher, written on the draft of a constitution for
the Druidical Encampment.

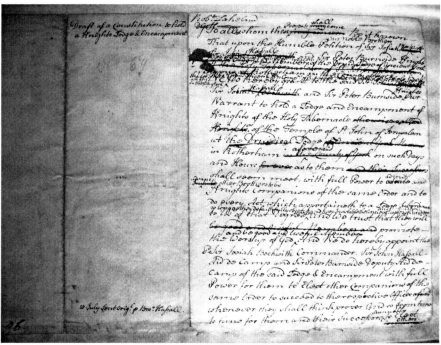

The rough draft of the constitution of the Knights Lodge
and Encampment at Druidical.

The letter from John Hassall, asking for assistance while he was held in
York Castle for debt.

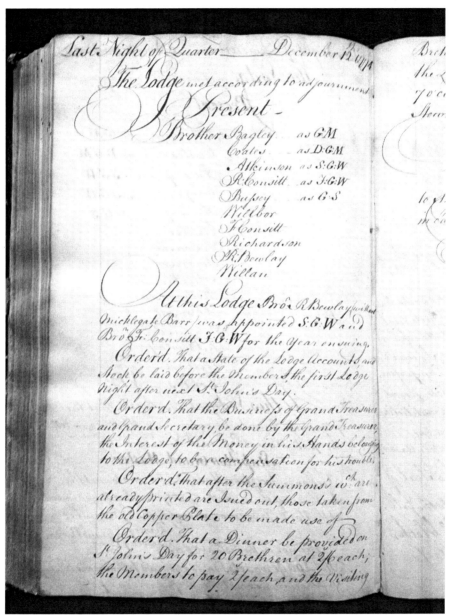

Last Night of Quarter ———— December 12 1774

The Lodge met according to adjournment

Present —

Brother Bagley .... as G.M
      Coates .... as D.G.M
      Atkinson as S.G.W
      R:Consitt as J.G.W
      Bussey .... as G.S
      Willbor
      F.Consitt
      Richardson
      R.Bewlay
      Willan

At this Lodge Bror. R Bewlay without Michlegate Barr, was appointed S.G.W and Bro. Fr: Consitt J.G.W for the Year ensuing.

Order'd. That a State of the Lodge Accounts and Stock be laid before the Members the first Lodge Night after next St. John's Day.

Order'd. That the Business of Grand Treasurer and Grand Secretary, be done by the Grand Treasurer, the Interest of the Money in his Hands belonging to the Lodge, to be a compensation for his trouble.

Order'd. That after the Summons's wch are already printed are Isued out, those taken from the old Copper Plate to be made use of

Order'd. That a Dinner be provided on St. John's Day for 20 Brethren at 2/ each; the Members to pay 2/ each, and the Visiting

The York Grand Lodge minute book, displaying a meeting on the 12th of December, 1774.

First Night of Quarter.

Monday 13 September 1779.

The Lodge assembled according to Adjournment.

Present

Wm. Siddall   G.M.

Edwd. Wolley as D.G.M.

Thos. Richardson as S.G.W.

Fra. Clubley as J.G.W.

John Browne G.S.

Fra. Consitt,

John Firth —,

Mr. Anthy. Robinson

John Hampston

John Hicks,

Wm. Smith,

Leon. Watson,

A fellow Crafts Lodge was opened, duly closed, and —
adjourned to the last Monday in this Month Except in
Case of Emergency.

Another study of the York Grand Lodge minute book, revealing a meeting on the
13th of September, 1779. Edward Wolley is featured as Deputy Grand Master.

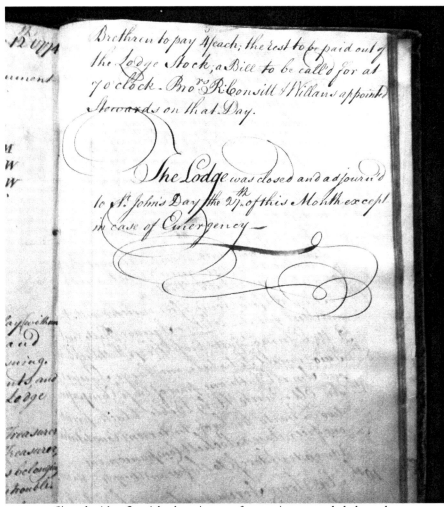

Brethren to pay 1/ each; the rest to be paid out of the Lodge Stock; a Bill to be call'd for at 7 o'clock. Bro.rs R: Consitt & Willans appointed Stewards on that Day.

The Lodge was closed and adjourn'd to St. John's Day the 27th. of this Month except in case of Emergency —

Signed with a flourish; the minutes of a meeting are ended elegantly.

Friday, July 10th 1795,

Being a regular Lodge Night, an Enter'd Apprentice Lodge was opened at the Crown Inn in East Retford, by Br. White as Master in the Chair, when the Minutes of the last Lodge Night were read by the Secy. — Br. the Revd. Beaumont Broadbent, Vicar of Stony Stainton & Maltby in Yorkshire, being of the Antient Masonry attended this Lodge, & requested to be made a Mason and raised to the third Degree according to our Form under the Grand Lodge of England, hoping that in consideration of his already being a Mason we

The Rev. Broadbent - a member of Druidical - had '*requested to be made a Mason and raised to the third Degree according to our form*', after visiting the North Nottinghamshire Lodge on the 10th of July, 1795. Evidence perhaps that Druidical had recently still been functioning

Chapter 5
The Expansion into Lancashire and the decline of the York Grand Lodge[197]

'We the K.T. of the R.E. No.15 do with all due submission write to acquaint you that on Tuesday Evening the 17th. Day of Octr. last such of us were Delegated and Authorised by you proceeded to open the G.R.E of all England in which we broke open and read our Warrant, constituted our R.E and installed our G.C.'
Letter describing the constitution of the Royal Encampment under York, held in Manchester, 1786.[198]

'...but no bro. Free Mason though otherwise ever so worthy, shall be admitted a member of the R.E. unless upon due examination he be found to have passed through the following important requisites...and has then but not till then been initiated into the R.A. and after that made a K.T. in this case he may be admitted into the R.E. but if upon examination it be found that he was made R.A. without such regular passing the chair or that he has been made a K.T. before a R.A. Mason in this case he must have his irregular steps regulated by repassing in due form or being remade...'
Doing it the York way; By-law No. 8 of the Royal Encampment under York.[199]

'...so that in every nation a Mason finds a friend, and in every climate a home.'
Thomas Smith Webb.[200]

Despite the ultimate failure of the Grand Lodge of England South of the River Trent, the sun had not quite set on York Freemasonry; even though the last complete minute book we have of the Grand Lodge ends in 1780, the Grand Lodge was still active, and certain Brethren under the York Grand Lodge were enthusiastic on expanding its influence into Lancashire. The lodge that established itself in Lancashire, according to Barker Cryer, was perhaps one of the last to survive out of the 'York' lodges, and according to new analysis of certain documents, the lodge may have lasted at least until 1802, though as we shall see, its influence certainly lasted much longer. A committed member of the York Grand Lodge, a certain Jacob Bussey, who had served as Grand

---

[197] Part of this chapter has previously appeared in the article; David Harrison, 'The Last Years of the York Grand Lodge – Part Two', in *The Journal of the Masonic Society*, the Masonic Society, Issue 23, (Spring, 2014).

[198] F.C. Shepherd & M.P. Lane, *Jerusalem Preceptory No. 5. Bi-centenary History 1786-1986*, (Manchester: Published by the Preceptory, 1986), p.17. Taken from the Minute books of the Jerusalem Preceptory No. 5, 1786-1795. Manchester Masonic Hall, Manchester. Not listed.

[199] Ibid., p.22.

[200] Thomas Smith Webb, *Webb's Freemason's Monitor*, (Cincinnati: C. Moore, 1865), p.8.

Secretary, moved to Manchester in 1779, but he died unexpectedly three years later, his death being mentioned in the *York Chronicle*.[201] John Hassall, the 'York' stalwart, who had previously been a founder of the Druidical Lodge, had moved to Manchester after his imprisonment for debt at York Castle, and it was Hassall who was to energetically spread the influence of the York Grand Lodge west of the Pennines.

Hassall first founded a Royal Encampment of Knights Templar in Manchester under the York Grand Lodge, which was constituted on the 10th of October, 1786, Hassall being the first Royal Grand Commander; an Office he held for five years. Interestingly, the original York Royal Encampment Warrant was numbered 15, hinting at administrative changes that had started with the numbering of Druidical Lodge some years before. This Royal Encampment of Knights Templar became extremely successful, though in 1795, it joined the Grand Encampment held in London under Thomas Dunkerley, the existing charter bearing the date of the 20th of May, 1795.[202] It seemed that Hassall was spreading the word of a different form of Freemasonry; and the interest in the five degrees of the York ritual was enough for the York Grand Lodge to obtain a tentative foothold in Lancashire. The Knights Templar was of course considered to be a fifth degree by the York Grand Lodge, and the hidden mysteries of this further 'degree' would undoubtedly be appealing to the more progressive Masons of Lancashire.

To form the Royal Encampment, Hassall appeared to have recruited a number of leading Brethren from Lodge No. 39; a Manchester based 'Antient' lodge that was to go through some sort of trouble a few years later. The petition for the Encampment was signed by Hassall on the 11th of June, 1786, along with a certain **Joseph Carter** and **John Watson**. Watson was a member of Lodge No. 39, and a few years later on the 28th of September, 1788, Watson, along with fellow lodge and original Royal Encampment members **John Hardman** and **James Cooper**, and 18 other members of No. 39, were 'remade' as Moderns, and allowed the warrant of No. 39 to lapse. Another original Royal Encampment member was James Ashton - a Manchester based shopkeeper who was a member of Lodge No. 196, another 'Antient' lodge that had recently moved to Bolton. Ashton had not signed the petition, but had signed the Encampment By-laws. **Richard Hunt** was also an original Encampment member and a member of Lodge No. 39. The attraction was obvious; to enter into the mysteries of a higher degree - a fifth degree offered under the York Grand Lodge - that of Knight Templar. Indeed, even today, the members of the Jerusalem Preceptory (now No. 5), which still meets in Manchester, are called

---

[201] See Johnson, *Subordinate Lodges*, p.133.

[202] See Gould, *The History of Freemasonry*, Vol.II, p.431, and see also John Masson, *Statutes of the Order of Masonic Knights Templar 1853*, (Kessinger Publishing, 2010), p.vi, which shows the Knights Templar Encampment named 'Jerusalem' that is based in Manchester.

'Sir Knight', akin to some Yorkshire Preceptories, as opposed to 'Brother Knight' which is used in the newer Preceptories in England.[203]

After forming the Encampment, Hassall then tried to get a Craft lodge under 'York' off the ground in Manchester, with a petition to form the lodge being forwarded to the York Grand Lodge on the 23rd of December, 1787 by four men including Hassall. This came to nothing, but two of the other men that had signed the petition - Thomas Daniel and John Broad - entered into the Royal Encampment.[204] Hassall then suddenly appeared as a visitor in the Oldham based Lodge of Friendship on the 17th of August, 1790. Oldham was a cotton producing town to the east of Manchester, and this 'Modern' lodge had only been founded the year before.

It seems that Hassall had been recruiting members for a new lodge under 'York', as the **Lodge of Fortitude** was founded soon after on the 27th of November, with Hassall and up to six leading brethren from the Oldham based 'Modern' lodge being involved, five of them being petitioners. Hassall certainly did not let Masonic prejudice get in the way of his recruitment process - both 'Antient' and 'Modern' Brethren being ready recruits for 'York' Masonry. The Lodge of Fortitude first met at The Sun, described as being located at the '*Bottom of Hollinwood*', near Oldham, the landlord of which, a certain James Taylor, had initially joined the Lodge of Friendship on the 2nd of September, 1789, becoming a 'full member' on the 23rd of February, the following year. Despite his obvious involvement in the 'York' lodge, he still visited his old lodge, with two recorded visits being on the 16th of March, 1791 (as a visitor from the Lodge of Integrity) and on the 20th of March, 1799.[205]

The five petitioners of Fortitude who came from the Lodge of Friendship included **Jonathan Raynor**, an Oldham weaver and founding member of Friendship who had been initiated into Lodge No. 354, an Irish lodge attached to the 49th Regiment, on the 7th of July, 1781. Raynor, as we shall see, cannily kept joint membership of both Friendship and Fortitude. Another petitioner; **Isaac Clegg**, who was a cotton manufacturer, was also a founding member of Friendship, and actually served as Worshipful Master in both the lodges at the same time, being the first to take the Chair in Fortitude. Clegg had also been a founding member of the Manchester based 'Modern' Union Lodge No. 534 in 1788, along with a number of other future members of the Lodge of

---

[203] For the fascinating early history of the Encampment see Shepherd & Lane, *Jerusalem Preceptory No. 5*, pp.5-27. See also the Minute books of the Jerusalem Preceptory No. 5, 1786-1795, Manchester Masonic Hall, Manchester. Not listed.

[204] Ibid, pp.12-13. John Broad entered on the 17th of April, 1787 and Thomas Daniel entered on the 17th of August, 1788.

[205] *List of Members of the Lodge of Friendship, no. 277, 2nd of September, 1789.* See also Fred L. Pick, 'The Lodge of Fortitude at Hollinwood', *MAMR*, Vol. LIII, (1963), pp.32-7.

Friendship.[206]   A further founding member of Friendship who was also a founding member of Fortitude was tailor **Samuel Brierley**, though unlike Raynor and Clegg, he resigned from Friendship.   Painter **Henry Mills**, also resigned from Friendship to serve as the first Senior Warden in Fortitude, but continued to visit his old lodge, as did weaver **John Booth**, who also resigned from Friendship.[207]

These visits from Fortitude continued to be indicated in the minutes of the Lodge of Friendship, for example a certain Brother James Whitehead from Fortitude attended on the 16th of February, 1791,[208] and another entry on the 5th of June, 1791, indicated that a certain John Scholfield was '*Renter'd from the Lodge of Fortitude*'.[209]   Whitehead continued to visit Friendship, next appearing while visiting with John Booth and William Fletcher on the 26th of August, 1795, the minutes indicating that they were from '*Hollinwood*', where of course, Fortitude was based.[210]   Whitehead returned later in the year on the 23rd of September with Fletcher and Michael Gunn, as did Booth, accompanied by Henry Mills on the 28th of October.[211]   These visits certainly point to Fortitude still being very active throughout 1795.

Jonathan Raynor, who had been the Lodge of Friendship's first Worshipful Master, visited Friendship on the 17th of December, 1791, when he was '*sencered for his bad behaviour...*'[212]   Despite this behavioural lapse, he remained a prominent figure in Friendship; he had served as Worshipful Master again in 1791 and 1795, and was always proposing candidates, though he seemed to fall on hard times, claiming relief from Friendship intermittently from November 1791, when he was advanced two guineas for the security of his watch, which was repaired and valued by another member.[213]   On the 27th of August, 1792, Raynor

---

[206] See Lane's Masonic Records <http://freemasonry.dept.shef.ac.uk/lane/> [accessed 9th of June, 2012]. The Lodge of Union No. 534 was constituted on the 27th of September, 1788, but was named the Union Lodge in 1792.

[207] See Fred L. Pick, 'The Lodge of Friendship No. 277 With Notes on Some Neighbouring Lodges and Chapters', *MAMR*, Vol. XXIII, (1933), pp.74-123, on pp.78-9. See also Fred L. Pick, 'Lodge of Friendship No. 277; A Link With The Grand Lodge Of All England, At York', *MAMR*, Vol.XXI, (1931), pp.149-154, on pp.150-1.

[208] *Minutes of the Lodge of Friendship, no. 277, 16th of February, 1791*. Masonic Hall, Rochdale. Not listed.

[209] Ibid., *5th of June, 1791*. See also Pick, 'Lodge of Fortitude', *MAMR*, Vol. LIII, p.35.

[210] *Minutes of the Lodge of Friendship, no. 277, 26th of August, 1795*. Masonic Hall, Rochdale. Not listed. See also Pick, 'Lodge of Fortitude', *MAMR*, Vol. LIII, p.35.

[211] Pick, 'Lodge of Fortitude', *MAMR*, Vol. LIII, p.35. In Pick's early paper on the 'Lodge of Friendship', in *MAMR*, Vol.XXI, p.153, he uses the 28th of August instead of the 26th as the date of Whitehead's visit, and on the same page, he uses the year 1803 instead of 1808 for Henry Mills' Office in Friendship as substitute Treasurer.

[212] *Minutes of the Lodge of Friendship, no. 277, 17th of December, 1791*. Masonic Hall, Rochdale. Not listed.

[213] Pick, 'The Lodge of Friendship', *MAMR*, Vol. XXIII, p.77.

was again given relief due to his '*his wife being ill a long time*'. His wife subsequently died, and Raynor remarried in 1793, but his hardships continued, and several monthly records appear in the Friendship cash book for his relief in early 1809.[214]

This closeness between the two lodges certainly gives an insight into the relationship between localised 'Modern' lodges and the 'York' lodge, reminding us that despite the antagonism between the two Grand Lodges, Freemasons from all backgrounds could still relate to each other at a local level. The visitor's book of the Lodge of Friendship records regular visitors by members of Fortitude up to the end of 1795, and as late as 1811, known members of Fortitude are still referred to; Henry Mills for example serving as substitute Treasurer on the 3rd of August, 1808, and Mills again serving as substitute Worshipful Master on the 9th of January, 1811, the year that Jonathan Raynor died. Raynor's funeral was mentioned by the Lodge of Friendship; a Lodge of Emergency was held on the 14th of April, 1811 '*for the Procession of our well-beloved Brother Jonathan Raynor*'. The lodge also paid £2 6s. for his coffin; Raynor, as a 'Modern' and York Mason was greatly missed.[215]

The lodge may have gradually faded away a number of years after Hassall's death in 1795, though with members still being mentioned as late as 1811, his influence may have lived on. A 'Modern' Royal Arch Chapter called the Chapter of Philanthropy was founded on the 13th of September, 1791, which met at the White Lion in Werneth, half way between Oldham and Hollinwood, and there were a number of active brethren from Hollinwood included, one of the founders being none other than Samuel Brierley. This Chapter was finally erased in 1839, and intriguingly a notebook was found and presented to the UGLE in 1963 which included the By-Laws of the Lodge of Fortitude, along with the By-Laws of the Royal Arch and a list of members involved in local Mark Masonry from 1790-1793. The list reveals eighteen local Mark members and it presents some recognisable names such as Samuel Brierley, James Taylor, John Booth and Michael Gunn, all linked to both Fortitude and Friendship.[216] One of the other members listed, a certain William Barlow was also a member of the Knights Templar St. Bernard's Conclave that had been founded at Hollinwood on the 1st of October, 1793.[217] The note book also includes extracts from the 1802 New York edition of Thomas Smith Webb's *Freemasons' Monitor*, which could suggest that the Lodge of Fortitude was still functioning at least

---

[214] *Minutes of the Lodge of Friendship, no. 277, 29th of March, 1809.* Masonic Hall, Rochdale. Not listed.

[215] See Pick, 'Lodge of Friendship', *MAMR*, Vol.XXI, pp.149-154. See also Burials for St. Mary's Church, Oldham, Jonathan Raynor, 14th of April, 1811, (Lancashire Record Office, Ref: DRM/2/239a/4).

[216] Pick, 'Lodge of Fortitude', *MAMR*, Vol. LIII, pp.35-7.

[217] Pick, 'Lodge of Friendship', *MAMR*, Vol. XXIII, pp.81-2, and Pick, 'Lodge of Fortitude', *MAMR*, Vol. LIII, p.37.

until that date, or at the very least insinuates that a member of Fortitude was still very interested in a variant form of Freemasonry.[218]

The lone 'York' Craft lodge in Lancashire which Hassall had instigated, certainly continued to have an impact on Masonry in the area; members of the lodge being active in local Freemasonry well into the first few decades of the nineteenth century, and its members influencing the continuation of Royal Arch and Mark Masonry in Oldham and Hollinwood. Further degrees were certainly of an interest to certain members of the Lodge of Friendship, with Thomas Taylor from Friendship, for example, joining the Manchester based Royal Encampment of Jerusalem in 1790.[219] Hassall was poorly educated, and it is a testament to his hard work that this lodge became not only one of the last bastions of the York Grand Lodge, but it firmly bridged the divide between 'Modern' and 'York' Masonry; Freemasons from different backgrounds working together and exploring and enjoying further degrees. The same can certainly be said of the Royal Encampment which included an eclectic mix of Masons from 'Antient' and 'Modern' lodges; there was a dynamic desire by keen Freemasons to search deeper into the hidden mysteries of nature and science, and to delve into a more Antient ceremony and research the higher degrees as practised by York.

However, another lodge was in the process of being constituted after the Lodge of Fortitude - its constitution being mentioned in the last ever minute entry we have of the York Grand Lodge on the 23rd of August, 1792, though which lodge in particular remains a mystery. Barker Cryer mentions that there was an opinion that this lodge could have been the **Lodge of Hope in Bradford**,[220] which still exists and has in its possession a version of the Old Charges, referred to as the old York Manuscript Constitution or the Hope MS, which has been dated to c.1680; Masonic historian William Hughan likening it to the York MS of 1693.[221] The Lodge of Hope however, was constituted under the 'Moderns', on the 23rd of March, 1794, although it had originally conferred

---

[218] 'Rules and orders, discretionary by-laws, laws respecting the R.A. sick fund, rules and orders of the R.A. Chapter, list of marks' for the Lodge of Fortitude, Hollinwood, UGLE, BE 167 FOR. The note book indicates that the extracts were taken from the 1802 edition of Thomas Smith Webb's *Freemasons' Monitor*. Webb's *Monitor* was heavily influenced by Preston's *Illustrations of Masonry*, and thus may have been popular with the York Masons of Fortitude. See the photograph of this notebook.

[219] See the list of members of the Encampment in Shepherd & Lane, *Jerusalem Preceptory No. 5*, p.54. See also *The List of Membership of the Lodge of Friendship, no. 277*. Thomas Taylor was a founding member of the lodge.

[220] See Barker Cryer, *York Mysteries*, p.374.

[221] Hughan, *Old Charges of British Freemasons*, p.12.
Also see
<http://www.rgle.org.uk/The%20old%20charges%20of%20British%20Freemasons%201872.pdf> [accessed 30th of May, 2012]

its Mark degree under the old York Manuscript Constitution.[222] In the Mark Register, which began in 1852, there is a list of certain Brethren that had been carried forward from a now lost older register, and amongst these names was Brother R.M. Scholefield, who was a Mark Mason from the Lodge of Hope during the opening decades of the nineteenth century. Scholefield was deputed by the lodge to attend the foundation of the UGLE in 1813 in order to ascertain the position of the Hope Mark degree under the new regulations, he then returned to Bradford with an arrangement that the Lodge of Hope could continue to practice the Mark degree as conferred by the old York Manuscript Constitution, which it still practiced independently until 1873 when it finally joined the Mark Grand Lodge, and still meets as the Old York TI Lodge.[223]

This instance of the Lodge of Hope Mark degree being conferred by a York Manuscript Constitution could be an example of a lodge, which in seeking higher degrees, was, like the brethren of the Lodge of Friendship in Oldham and the Royal Encampment in Manchester, able to cross the Grand Lodge divide without prejudice. There seems to be a consensus within the history of the Lodge of Hope that the lodge may be related to an older working lodge in the area, and despite being constituted as a 'Modern' lodge, it is clear that there was an influence from the York Grand Lodge. At the first meeting of the Lodge of Hope, a number of Brethren visited from the Lodge of Harmony, a 'Modern' lodge which was based in Halifax and had been warranted in 1789.[224]

Certain Hope Brethren had previously been members of Harmony, and it has been theorised by the Yorkshire Masonic historian C.J. Scott, that various Bradford Masons under the York Grand Lodge could have gone through a re-making ceremony in the Lodge of Harmony and went on to found the Lodge of Hope in Bradford - the location of a gathering of Masons under York in 1713. No evidence has yet come to light of this, but as a theory, it attempts to explain how the Lodge of Hope may have come to possess the old York Manuscript Constitution, and how they came to practice the Mark degree. The Brethren of Hope could thus be members of a larger Masonic networking community as a

---

[222] See Waite, *Secret Tradition in Freemasonry*, pp.46-7. See also <http://www.markmastermasonscornwall.org.uk/history-of-mark-master-masons> [accessed 30th of May, 2012]

[223] See Bernard H. Springett, *The Mark Degree*, (London: A. Lewis, 1968), pp.15-17. Springett comments in the history section of the book that early Mark Masonry was worked in Yorkshire, and presents evidence that it was also practiced in the Marquis of Granby Lodge No. 124 in Durham, in 1773. Springett also theorises that the Mark degree may have been taken to the south of England by Thomas Dunkerley.

[224] For information on the Lodge of Harmony in Halifax, which still meets today in Huddersfield, see Hanson, *Lodge of Probity*, pp.124-125.

'Modern' lodge, but with the possession of the old York Manuscript Constitution, they could have the ancient right to practice other degrees.[225]

There was however, another group of Freemasons who termed themselves *'Made as York Masons'* residing in Wigan, who subsequently joined the 'Modern' Lodge of Sincerity; ten in all from 1789-1802. All were from Wigan, except one who was from nearby Ashton, which suggests that these ten brethren were local, and could have originally joined a lodge in the Wigan area which had a 'York' influence. There are no other records of a 'York' lodge being established so far into Lancashire, and certainly no record of such within the York Grand Lodge minutes, but there was an 'Antient' lodge in Wigan called the **Lodge of Antiquity** which termed its members as *'York Masons'*.[226]

All ten of these *'York Masons'* that had joined the Lodge of Sincerity, had previously been members of this Wigan based Lodge of Antiquity, a lodge formed in 1786; its early minutes proudly referring to the York legend of Prince Edwin. It was not uncommon for 'Antient' lodges to refer to the York legend in their warrant, or indeed to refer to their members as 'York' Masons, but the fact that the members of Antiquity referred to themselves so strongly as being *'Made as York Masons'* when joining a 'Modern' lodge, hints at a possible 'York' influence to their original lodge working. Indeed, the Lodge of Antiquity was, up until 1860, named the Antient Royal Arch Lodge, suggesting that, as an 'Antient' lodge, they practiced the Royal Arch 'degree' within the confines of the lodge, and not in a separate Chapter as the 'Modern' lodges did.[227]

The first of the ten *'York Masons'* to join Sincerity was named William Hilton; an Innkeeper from Wigan, and he had originally joined Antiquity on the 2nd of October, 1786. He then went on to join Sincerity on the 24th of May, 1789, a note in the *'Remarks'* column of the Sincerity membership book stating that he was *'Made by the York masons but joined the English Constn'*, a statement which seems to suggest he was a member of a lodge under the York Grand Lodge but then joined either a 'Modern' or 'Antient' lodge. The second of these *'York Masons'* was Thomas Hilton (or Halton), a hairdresser from Wigan, he had

---

[225] C.J. Scott, *The Tradition of The Old York T. I. Lodge of Mark Master Masons: An enquiry into early Freemasonry at Bradford and neighborhood 1713-1873.* A paper given before the Old York T.I. Lodge at Bradford on November 28th, 1911. Scott was the Chaplain to the Old York T.I. Lodge.

<http://www.bradford.ac.uk/webofhiram/?section=york_rite&page=tradoldyork.html> [accessed 30th of October, 2013]

[226] *A List of the Members of the Lodge of Sincerity No. 402, 29th of January, 1787 – 5th of September, 1821.* Pemberton Masonic Hall, Wigan. Not Listed. This document is a Photostat copy of a now lost membership list of Sincerity. It does however correspond to the original transcribed by Norman Rogers in his paper 'The Lodge of Sincerity, No. 1 of The Wigan Grand Lodge', in *AQC*, Vol. LXII, (1951), pp.33-76. Also see J. Brown, *Masonry in Wigan being a brief history of the Lodge of Antiquity No. 178, Wigan, originally No. 235,* (Wigan: R. Platt, Standishgate and Millgate, 1882), p.55. Brown put forward in the history that 'Atholl' lodges did sometimes refer its members as *'York Masons'*, on p.16.

[227] Ibid.

joined Antiquity in 1787, and joined Sincerity on the 21st of February, 1793, the 'Remarks' column firmly stating in the present tense that he was 'A York Mason'. Interestingly, a Freemason who had joined Sincerity in 1794 was described as 'An ancient Mason', though he was not previously a member of Antiquity. After July 1799, the other eight of the ten brethren are described as being 'formerly' York Masons, a reference perhaps to the recent demise of the York Grand Lodge, or maybe just the particular way of referring to their status as being formerly a member of Antiquity.[228]

The Lodge of Antiquity was constituted on the 21st of June 1786, by Brethren from none other but Lodge No. 39 in Manchester and Lodge No. 196 in Bolton - along with a member from Lodge No. 171 in Salford who was also present at the constitution. All these were 'Antient' Lodges based in Lancashire, and Lodge No. 39 in particular, as we have seen, had an interesting link to the York Grand Lodge; around the same time that the Lodge of Antiquity was founded in Wigan, certain members of Lodge No. 39 along with John Hassall, had signed a petition addressed to the York Grand Lodge for the 'Warrant of the Jerusalem Encampment of Knight Templar, the first and premier encampment of all Lancashire'.[229] John Watson, who had served as Worshipful Master of Lodge No. 39 for six months from December 1785, John Hardman also of Lodge No. 39 and James Ashton of Lodge No. 196, all of whom were to be present at the first meeting of the Royal Encampment, were all in attendance for the constitution of the Lodge of Antiquity in Wigan.[230] It seems that this may be an example of certain Freemasons in Lancashire seeking access to further degrees as practised by 'York' and inspiring the working of other lodges in their area.

Lodge No. 171 also had a 'York' connection; a certain Peter Berside had moved to Lodge No. 171 after petitioning for a 'York' Lodge at Doncaster in 1779 - a tenuous link perhaps, but it does reveal how Masons of 'York' persuasion had moved into Lancashire and may have inspired elements of a York stylisation and fashion within certain lodges.[231] All the ten 'York Masons' were local to the Wigan area, and seemed to have been initiated into Antiquity as it is indicated in the Antiquity membership lists when a particular Mason was a new or joining member.[232] Lodge No. 171 in Salford ceased in 1793; according to Lane's Masonic Records, the warrant was cancelled due to the lodge taking a 'Modern' constitution. Another Lodge No. 171 was constituted in Bury in 1803 and was later called the Prince Edwin Lodge, celebrating the York Edwin

---

[228] Ibid. See also *A List of the Members of the Lodge of Sincerity No. 402, 29th of January, 1787 – 5th of September, 1821*. Pemberton Masonic Hall, Wigan. Not Listed.

[229] Norman Rogers, *Two Hundred Years of Freemasonry in Bolton*, (MAMR, 1941), p.48.

[230] Shepherd & Lane, *Jerusalem Preceptory No. 5*, pp.12-14 and Brown, *Masonry in Wigan*, p.10

[231] Brown, *Masonry in Wigan*, p.55.

[232] None of the ten 'York Masons' of Antiquity appear on the membership list of the Royal Encampment in Manchester.

legend.[233]   Interestingly, lodges under the Provincial Grand Lodge of Pennsylvania in the US, warranted through the 'Antients' in England in 1761, also styled themselves as Ancient York Masons.[234]

The Lodge of Sincerity went on to become the leading lodge in the rebel Grand Lodge of Wigan, forged from the Liverpool Masonic Rebellion of 1823, and even though it was disallowed to discuss the United Grand Lodge during their meetings, and almost unheard of that they would accept visitors from lodges under the UGLE, it is recorded that they had visitors from Yorkshire during a meeting on the 14th of September, 1867.[235] It was not recorded what actual lodge the Yorkshire Brethren came from, but Sincerity was certainly open to Freemasons who were of more 'Antient' and flexible persuasions. Like the York Grand Lodge, the Wigan Grand Lodge practised the Royal Arch as a separate degree, and they also worked the Knights Templar and Mark 'degrees'.

The End of the York Grand Lodge

William Blanchard became the last surviving member of the York Grand Lodge, and was the custodian of the minutes and documents of the York Grand Lodge after its demise. He became the main source of information for Masonic historians in the early nineteenth century, and a number of sources mention him, or a member of his family as supplying documents; local historian G. Benson mentioned that it was a 'Captain Blanchard' who presented the Records of the York Grand Lodge to the York based 'Union' Lodge in 1837,[236] though in the official history of the lodge, William Blanchard himself is cited as presenting many of the records to the Union Lodge in 1817.[237] Blanchard apparently gave the Grand Lodge Board (painted by Thomas Beckwith back in 1778) to a Bro. Turner of the 'Union' Lodge, and Arthur Edward Waite revealed that Blanchard

---

[233] See Lane's Masonic Records <http://www.hrionline.ac.uk/lane> [accessed 12th of June, 2013] For recent information on lodges in Bolton and their social makeup see the work of David Hawkins, *Membership of the 'Anchor and Hope' Lodge, Bolton, 1732-1813*, a paper presented to the ICHF, 2009.

[234] Anon., *Ahiman Rezon, containing a view of the history and polity of Free Masonry together with the rules and regulations of the Grand Lodge and of the Grand Holy Royal Arch Chapter of Pennsylvania*, (Philadelphia: Grand Lodge of Pennsylvania, 1825), p.74. The history presented here also puts forward an interesting set of events in South Carolina; how a desire to form a Grand Lodge there by '*York masons*', led to '*four lodges of ancient York Masons*' – three of which held warrants from the Grand Lodge of Pennsylvania, and a lodge that belonged to the '*grand lodge of ancient free masons of England and not to the York Masons*' into coming together to form the Grand Lodge for South Carolina in January 1787. The use of the 'York' name here seems to reflect the use of the Edwin legend by the 'Antient' Grand Lodge of Pennsylvania.

[235] See Harrison, *The Liverpool Masonic Rebellion and the Wigan Grand Lodge*, p.72. Taken from the transcribed Lodge of Sincerity minutes in; Rogers, 'The Lodge of Sincerity, No. 1', *AQC*, Vol. LXII, p.48.

[236] G. Benson, *John Browne 1793-1877, Artist and the Historian of York Minster*. (York: Yorkshire Philosophical Society, 1918), p.5.

[237] Wood, *York Lodge*, p.33.

was the source for the mysterious documents seen by Godfrey Higgins, and mentioned that Blanchard had given documents and papers to local York historian William Hargrove. Gould in his *History of Freemasonry* also mentions Hargrove seeing the 1780-1792 minute book in the hands of Blanchard in 1819.[238] Whatever the story, like James Miller - the last surviving Mason under the Wigan Grand Lodge over a century later, Blanchard became much sought after for information concerning the York Grand Lodge, as it soon became swathed in Masonic mystery.

In the first minute book of the Manchester based Jerusalem Preceptory, there is an interesting copy letter dated the 8th of July, 1791, which gives an indication of the dire state that the York Grand Lodge was in. The letter from Br. George Kitson of York and addressed to '*Mr. Hassall*', concerns the application of warrants for further degrees by the Encampment, and the obvious lack of activity in York:

'*...you have so long been disappointed of your warrants. The illness of our G.M. and the absence of our Deputy G. Who has been long in London is the reason of our delay – Bro. Wooley I am told will soon return and as our G.M. is a little better, I hope very soon we shall hold a Chapter and a RE and then the Secy will have orders to prepare and send you the warrants.*'

It seems that the lack of communication persisted as on the 14th of April, 1793, five members of the Encampment were nominated to visit '*Mr. Singelair*'. This was obviously a reference to Robert Sinclair, and in the July, the expenses of a Brother sent to York were paid, and it seemed that some kind of a discussion took place - either concerning the warrants or to discuss the future of the Encampment in light of the decline of the York Grand Lodge. Either way, on the 20th of May, 1795, the Encampment had a new warrant under the Dunkerley Grand Encampment and entered into a new phase in its history.[239]

We can say that the York Grand Lodge, in accordance to the available documentation, continued officially until 1792, but, as we have seen, its last two subordinate lodges lasted slightly longer; the Druidical lodge in Rotherham lasting to around 1795 and the Lodge of Fortitude in Hollinwood, Lancashire, operating perhaps as late as 1802. When examining the local York based 'Modern' 'Union' Lodge, the influence of the Grand Lodge may have even survived into the early years of the nineteenth century, with some of the surviving York Grand Lodge members, such as Blanchard, the last known Grand Master Edward Wolley, Robert Sinclair and especially the Rev. John Parker, interacting with and visiting the 'Union' Lodge - the 'York' members being well received by a local 'Modern' lodge which had been founded on the principles of union.

---

[238] Gould, *History of Freemasonry*, Vol.II, p.419.

[239] Shepherd & Lane, *Jerusalem Preceptory No. 5*, pp.26-7.

According to the history of the York 'Union' Lodge, certain leading members of the York Grand Lodge had subsequently joined the Union Lodge, such as Brother J. Consitt who joined *'after the demise of the York Grand Lodge'* and his brother R. Consitt who joined in 1789.[240] However, when the last known Grand Master Edward Wolley visited the York 'Union' Lodge on the 27th of August, 1802, he signed himself as a member of the York Grand Lodge. The Rev. John Parker visited the York 'Union' Lodge a total of 25 times between 1802-1814, and he was regularly referred to in the minutes as the *'Grand Chaplain'* to the York Grand Lodge.[241] It was the Rev. Parker who seemed to have especially endeared himself to the 'Union' Lodge, first appearing at a Lodge of Emergency where he conducted the ceremony for the burial of a Brother Dunn on the 10th of March, 1802.[242] The Reverend was duly thanked by the lodge in a letter, and during a meeting on the 1st of June that year for *'The Thanksgiving for the Blessings of Peace'*, he accompanied the lodge on a procession, giving a much thanked discourse, and was later joined by fellow York Grand Lodge member Robert Sinclair.[243]

The Rev. Parker continued to visit quite regularly, seemingly being adopted by the local 'Modern' Lodge; the Reverend being invited to preach appropriate sermons at the Parish Church of St. Helen's after processions by the lodge, such as the one proposed by the Master on the interment of Lord Nelson on the 16th of December, 1805, and the procession on the 7th of July, 1814, to celebrate the peace following the Napoleonic War. Parker's death and burial in the June of 1815, at the age of 74, was mentioned in the *York Courant*, where the good Reverend was referred to as *'being Grand Chaplain in the Grand Lodge of all England, to the Provincial Grand Lodge of York, and the Apollo and Union Lodges'*, and that *'several of the fraternity were present.'*[244] Parker had also evidently endeared himself to the York based Apollo Lodge, having conducted the burial service for the ex-

---

[240] Wood, *York Lodge*, p.31 and p.122.

[241] Minute Books of the York 'Union' Lodge No. 236, number 10 and 11. See also Barker Cryer, *York Mysteries*, p.351-2.

[242] Minutes of the Union Lodge, York, No. 236, Book 10, January 1796-December 1808, 10th of March, 1802. Duncombe Place, York.

[243] Ibid, 1st of June, 1802. The entry refers to a *'Br. Sinclair'* honouring the lodge with his company, but it seems obvious that this is Robert Sinclair who is being referred to, and Masonic historian and Librarian of the York 'Union' Lodge G.Y. Johnson indicated this confidently in his transcription of the minutes. See the photo of this entry. Also see Appendix III which lists the visits of the Rev. Parker, Edward Wolley and Robert Sinclair to the York 'Union' Lodge. There was also a *'Bro. Sinclair'* who visited the Lennox Lodge No. 123, in Richmond, in July, 1812. Barker Cryer states that Sinclair visited the York 'Union' Lodge twice in 1802; see Barker Cryer, *York Mysteries*, p.351.

[244] Wood, *York Lodge*, p.18. The death of the Rev. Parker is reported in the *York Courant* on Monday, the 19th of June, 1815, and his burial on Monday, the 25th of June, 1815.

York Grand Secretary John Browne while Brethren of the Apollo Lodge had attended and taken part in the ceremony.[245]

Interestingly, with the decline of the York Grand Lodge, the Provincial Grand Lodge of Yorkshire had started to meet regularly once more after December 1803, becoming more pro-active, and in October 1805, the Hon. Lawrence Dundas became Deputy Provincial Grand Master. Dundas had been present at the meeting of the York 'Union' Lodge on the 27th of August, 1802, when Edward Wolley and the Rev. Parker had attended, and Dundas went on to become the first Provincial Grand Master of the newly created Province of the North and East Ridings of Yorkshire, being installed on the 14th of August, 1821.[246] The large Yorkshire Province had been split in two in 1817 to make it more manageable, a move which, in light of the rebellion that was to come in Lancashire, was very wise.

It can be said that the spirit of the York Grand Lodge was still very much alive with the activities of prominent members such as Sinclair, Wolley and the Rev. Parker, who, incidentally, did not join any other lodge. It seemed that the essence of the York Grand Lodge at least, may have indeed continued into the early decades of the nineteenth century, its embers finally dying with the last of its members.

---

[245] Barker Cryer, *York Mysteries*, pp.434-5.

[246] Albert Morton, Lennox Lodge No.123, (Richmond: 1947), pp.15-21. The Hon. Lawrence Dundas (became a joining member of the York 'Union' Lodge in September 1802 and a subscribing member of the Lennox Lodge (based in Richmond, Yorkshire) in December 1830. The Dundas family became embedded with nineteenth and Twentieth century English Freemasonry; the Hon. Thomas Dundas (afterwards the 2nd Earl of Zetland) becoming Provincial Grand Master of the North and East Ridings of Yorkshire in 1834, and serving as Grand Master from 1844-1870.

March 10th 1802 – A Lodge of Emergency called
for the express purpose of attending Br. Adams
Funeral – A Member of the Rodney Lodge. (all)
Apprentice Lodge opened

Pres.t the W.M – S.S. J.W. & the Officers of the
Union Lodge – the rest of the Brothers of the same
Lodge and Visitors to the N.o of 52 in all –

the Rev.d Mr. Parker Chaplain to the Grand Lodge of
all England attended and performed the Ceremony
after which the Lodge was closed until the
11th of March except in Case of Emergency

The minutes of the York 'Union' Lodge indicating that the Rev. John Parker attended as Chaplain of the Grand Lodge of all England on the 10th of March, 1802.

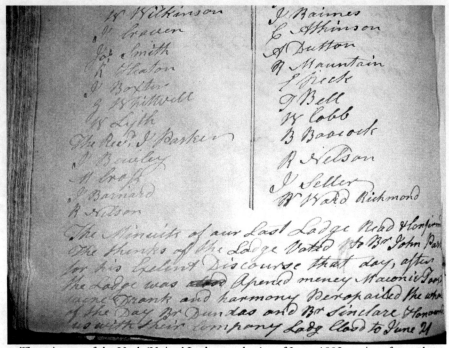

The minutes of the York 'Union' Lodge on the 1st of June, 1802, again refer to the Rev. Parker visiting along with Bro. Sinclair.

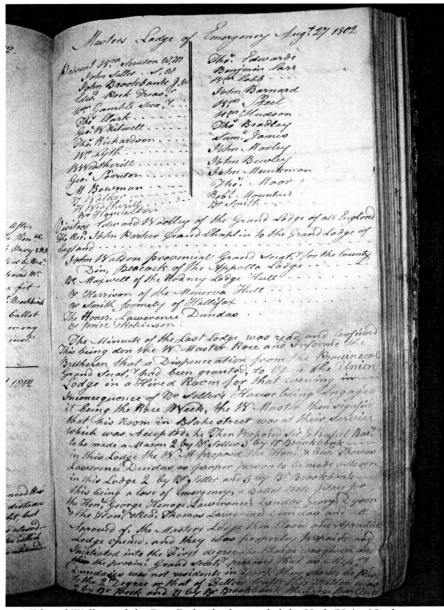

Edward Wolley and the Rev. Parker both attended the York 'Union' Lodge on the 27th of August, 1802, as members of the Grand Lodge of all England.

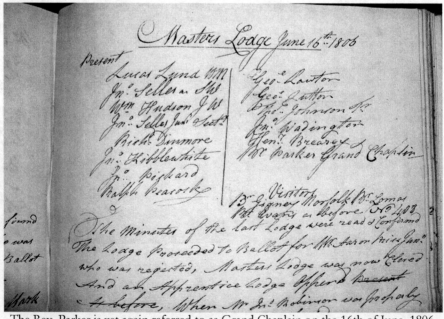

The minutes of the York 'Union' Lodge on the 21st of June, 1803, again refer to the Rev. Parker as G.C.

The Rev. Parker is yet again referred to as Grand Chaplain on the 16th of June, 1806. The title was obviously still recognised at this late stage.

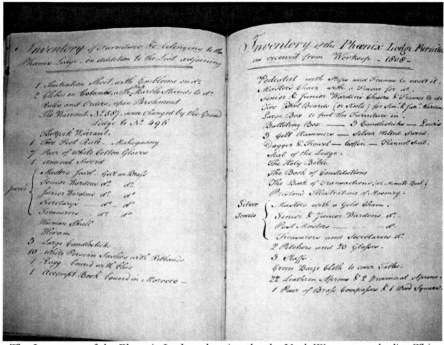

The Inventory of the Phoenix Lodge, showing the the York Warrant on the list. This was the Warrant of Druidical Lodge, and a number of surviving Druidical members joined the new lodge with members of North Nottinghamshire Lodge in 1808. A human skull is also on the list, revealing its use in the third degree ceremony.

The page from the Lodge of Fortitude By-laws that reveals the hand copied text of
Thomas Smith Webb's 'Monitor', as taken from the New York 1802 edition,
as indicated at the bottom of the page. It certainly suggests that a member of
Fortitude was still interested in a more independent form of Freemasonry,
and may hint that the lodge was still functioning.
(Photo taken by Martin Cherry, care of the Library and Museum of the UGLE)

Conclusion

The York Grand Lodge, though only termed a Grand Lodge after 1726, was certainly borne from an older, local body, one that was established and important enough to attract the local gentry to become directly involved, such as Sir Walter Hawkesworth and Robert Fairfax. From Drake's speech of 1726, we can ascertain that the Grand Lodge still affiliated itself with working Masons and the trades of the city, suggesting that a relationship between 'speculative' and 'operative', albeit at a social level, still existed. The adoption of the Grand Lodge title was indeed a bold statement; York taking a defiant stand against the growing power of the London based Grand Lodge. In this sense, the York Grand Lodge assisted in forging a local cultural identity; an indigenous pride that can also be seen in the development of York's civil buildings during the eighteenth century, such as the Assembly Rooms.

The working used by the early York 'Grand Lodge' can only be glimpsed at through the incidents of lodge meetings such as the ones that took place at Scarborough in 1705, Bradford in 1713 and Leeds in 1721, where a number of gentlemen were 'admitted' at once; special lodges set up for this purpose which used versions of the 'Old Charges', the gentlemen being admitted as apprentices and fellow-crafts at the same meeting. But like the Freemasonry practiced under the Premier Grand Lodge in London - York Masonry was also going through flux; as seen not only with its adoption of the Grand Lodge title, but also in the development of its ritual.[247] The mention of Royal Arch Masons in York by Dassigny in 1744 and the later use of five degrees at York by the late 1770s, point to a progressive evolution of the York ritual throughout the eighteenth century. Freemasons certainly wanted access to further degrees in an effort to search for the hidden mysteries of nature and science. Certainly at the revival of the Grand Lodge in 1761, the Brethren from the 'Modern' Punch Bowl lodge seemed to merge easily with Drake and his fellow original 'York' members, suggesting that the Craft tri-gradal system, as practiced by the 'Moderns' was at this time recognised by 'York'.

After its revival, the York Grand Lodge experienced success; lodges were founded, the Grand Lodge of England south of the River Trent came under the sway of York, and its influence spread into Lancashire, overcoming not just the age-old county rivalries but the rivalries of the Grand Lodges themselves. The strong and professional administration along with a unique ritual that, by the late 1770s, extended to five degrees, undoubtedly aided in attracting certain Freemasons, which can be seen in the founding of the Royal Encampments at Rotherham and Manchester, and the relative successes of the Druidical and

---

[247] Barker Cryer, *York Mysteries*, p.269.

Fortitude lodges. However, it was not to last, and the fabric of the York Grand Lodge began to fray in the 1790s.

In all, a pattern developed in regard to the fate of the lodges under the York Grand Lodge; they either faded away quickly, or seemed to be replaced by new lodges; mainly under the 'Modern' Grand Lodge, such as the Druidical Lodge in Rotherham which, after its demise, witnessed five 'York' brethren being members of the Phoenix Lodge; the Ripon Lodge which was 'replaced' by the Royal Oak Lodge, which met at the same Inn and had four members from the local 'York' lodge, and the Knaresborough Lodge which was 'replaced' by the Newtonian Lodge, which again had at least four members from the previous local 'York' lodge. The early York lodge at Halifax had been quickly 'replaced' by the 'Modern' Lodge of Probity, hinting at the fate of its later subordinate lodges.

Perhaps the localised York Grand Lodge was too limited for the networking ambitions of its Brethren; the limitations of visiting other lodges and being part of a larger Masonic community becoming more apparent. Nevertheless, the York working, and the ability to share the working of higher degrees was still an attraction to various 'Modern' and 'Antient' Masons in Yorkshire and Lancashire, and this ultimately led to a continued 'York' legacy in certain areas, such as the Mark degree attached to the Lodge of Hope in Bradford and the Royal Encampment of Knights Templar in Manchester.

The York Grand Lodge had somewhat apparent paradoxical ideals; York boasted ancient traditions and it claimed to be the original source of English Freemasonry. However, it practiced a seemingly progressive five degree system by the late 1770s, a system that appealed to both 'Antient' and 'Modern' Masons. As the renowned Masonic writer Arthur Edward Waite would put forward over a century later *'there is a Masonry which is behind Masonry and is not commonly communicated in lodges, though at the right time it is made known to the right person'*,[248] a comment which would have resounded with English Freemasons at the time of the York Grand Lodge, and with a pro-active York Mason such as John Hassall appearing in Lancashire and willing to offer an enlightened pathway to further degrees, it is not surprising that a Royal Encampment of Knights Templar and a new Craft lodge not only took root, but continued to influence certain Masons in the area.

Indeed, the desire to explore further degrees and to continue the search for the hidden mysteries of nature and science was commonplace during the later eighteenth century, but the allure of further degrees along with the ancient customs of York would certainly have been an attractive package for some Masons. The 'York' name itself seemed to represent an independent style of working, and indeed, the pride in being termed a *'York Mason'* can clearly be seen

---

[248] See R.A. Gilbert, 'The Masonic Career of A.E. Waite', in *AQC*, Vol.99, (1986). See also Harrison, *Transformation of Freemasonry*, pp.165-6.

in the ten members of the Wigan based Lodge of Antiquity who joined the 'Modern' Lodge of Sincerity from 1789-1802.

Despite this, the decline of the York Grand Lodge was irreversible by the end of the eighteenth century; with York unable to compete with the greater networking opportunities that the 'Moderns' and the 'Antients' could offer the younger ambitious brethren. The 1799 Unlawful Societies Act may have become the final death knell for any revival of the York Grand Lodge; unprotected by the oppressive legislation, unlike the 'Modern', 'Antient' and the Scottish Grand Lodges, and affected by the subsequent downturn of Freemasonry in the wake of the Act, the few active York Grand Lodge members themselves, though indicating with pride their status, visited the leading 'Modern' lodge in the city, and continued to enjoy their Freemasonry in the security of the York 'Union' Lodge. It is also interesting that of the ten members of the Wigan based Lodge of Antiquity who had termed themselves *'York Masons'* when joining Sincerity, those that joined after 1799 were termed as being *'formerly York Masons'*. Was this perhaps a new mode of description, or was this pointing to the fact that the scribe believed that the York Grand Lodge had all but ended by then? Either way, by this time, the end was nigh.

Throughout its later life, the York Grand Lodge continued to include prominent local gentlemen, such as William Siddall Esq., who served as Mayor the same year he served as Grand Master in 1783, Sir Thomas Gascoigne, Bart., and William Blanchard, who was the last Grand Secretary, and owned the York Chronicle. Indeed, as with the Wigan Grand Lodge later in the nineteenth century, intelligent and dedicated Freemasons such as Dr Francis Drake, William Blanchard and Robert Sinclair - because of their location in the north of England, or perhaps because of their political persuasions, may never have had a chance to work at Grand Lodge level for the 'Moderns' or even the 'Antients'. Their work in constituting lodges, conducting their own ritual and organising and administrating a professionally run Grand Lodge at York, in the face of opposition from the 'Modern' and 'Antient' Grand Lodges, was a testament to their dedication. Tradesmen and working class men such as John Hassall, a devoted York Freemason who worked tirelessly founding new lodges despite being poorly educated and being imprisoned for debt, may never have had the chance to have been so trusted in establishing lodges and even Royal Encampments, if he was a Mason under the 'Modern' or 'Antient' Grand Lodges.

The 'Union' Lodge was founded in York in 1777 by both 'Antient' and 'Modern' Freemasons and became a bastion to the memory of the York Grand Lodge.[249] According to the official 'Union' Lodge history, the brethren were still using the *'York Working'* of the ritual in 1822 when the lodge finally agreed to adopt the new system, as taught by the Lodge of Reconciliation, which had been

---

[249] The York Grand Lodge documents which intermittently date from the 19th of March, 1712 and end on the 23rd of August, 1792, are in the possession of the York 'Union' Lodge.

set up by the UGLE. Despite this, the 'Union' Lodge decided to continue the *'York Working'* as no member of the lodge had seen the new system demonstrated.[250] The York architectural historian John Browne, who joined the Union Lodge in 1825, was heavily influenced by Antient York Masonry and studied the Antient ritual, and the lodge still uses the *'York Working'* today. In the current York Working Ritual Book, it states *'that the Ritual used in the York Lodge is most likely to be that of the "Moderns" with perhaps a little influence from the "Antients" and possibly some from the Grand Lodge of All England'*, and as the York 'Union' Lodge had regular visitors from the York Grand Lodge, and it became the home for the York relics, it is no surprise that certain elements of the York Grand Lodge ritual seeped into this 'Modern' lodge.[251]

In a similar fashion to its earlier manifestation, the revived York Grand Lodge seemed unable to sustain its initial momentum, and finding it hard to compete with both the 'Moderns' and the 'Antients', it faded away, a rapid decline taking place from the 1790s.[252] However, the influence of the York Grand Lodge survived, especially with the continuation to the present day of the Royal Encampment of Knights Templar in Manchester that was originally under York and the practice of the Mark 'degree' conferred by York at the Lodge of Hope in Bradford. Former members under 'York' lodges at Rotherham and Hollinwood were active in various other lodges until the first few decades of the nineteenth century and the memory of York Masonry with its independent ritual and outlook continues to fascinate Masonic historians today.

Postscript
In December 2005, around 200 years after the York Grand Lodge had disappeared; a group of Freemasons came together and called themselves the Grand Lodge of All England held at York. A convocation of the Grand Lodge took place at Bedern Hall at York on the 12th of June, 2006, preceded by a meeting of St. John's Lodge; the Grand Lodge installing, investing and proclaiming its Grand Master Elect John Gordon Graves, who then invested his Grand Officers.[253] The Grand Lodge had, for a brief number of years, a rather active online presence, with an impressive website and lively discussions on certain forums, where their Grand Secretary - actor Peter J. Clatworthy - put forward how the 'revived' Grand Lodge was based, like the old York Grand

---

[250] Wood, *York Lodge*, p.20.

[251] Anon., *York Working of the Masonic Ritual compiled from manuscript records in the possession of the York Lodge No. 236*, (York: Ben Johnson & Co., 1981), p.2.

[252] Gould, *History of Freemasonry*, Vol.II, pp.419-21. Also see Waite, *New Encyclopaedia of Freemasonry*, Vol.II, p.482.

[253] The records of Bedern Hall, York, reveal that a meeting did take place on this date, organised by the Grand Secretary Peter J. Clatworthy. The existing manager of the Hall still remembers the meeting as a dinner event with attendees from all over the country.

Lodge, on the Edwin legend and, in essence, that they were a legitimate revival.[254]

However, they soon attracted criticism, and despite a new lodge called St. John's Lodge being founded in Dayton, Ohio in the US on the 21st of November 2007,[255] and a reported meeting held in the Crypt of York Minster in June 2008, where the Grand Master received 'The Order of Service to Freemasonry' from the Chancellor of The Grand Loge De France, Jean-Claude Hertz,[256] they had completely disappeared from the internet by 2010. However, they are still very much in operation at the time of writing and still claim to be a constitutional restoration of the Grand Lodge of All England.[257]

It appears that the basis of this new Grand Lodge is in the revival of the constitution and principles of the old York Grand Lodge, similar to the revival witnessed in 1761, though back then of course, actual surviving members of the original Grand Lodge were directly involved. Indeed, only four members of this new organisation were ever publically mentioned online,[258] though there seemed to be many more that were active privately.[259] However, this rather interesting twist does signify how the York Grand Lodge continues to inspire; its title, its

---

[254] See Trevor W. McKeown, 'An historical outline of freemasons online', Grand Lodge of British Columbia and Yukon, (2008), p.31. McKeown certainly notes the coincidence with the founding of the independent Regular Grand Lodge of England in January 2005 and the founding of the Grand Lodge of All England later that year. Indeed, correspondence between myself and Rui Gabirro, who was a leading member of the Regular Grand Lodge of England, confirmed that the Masons behind the formation of the Grand Lodge of All England had been involved with Masons from the Regular Grand Lodge of England, which also incidentally, uses the Edwin legend on its website.

[255] See <http://freemasonsfordummies.blogspot.co.uk/2007/11/another-lodge-appears.html> [accessed on the 4th of April, 2014]. The website is managed by Christopher Hodapp, the US based author of Freemasons for Dummies.

[256] The Grand Loge De France is not recognised by the UGLE, but they do have a lodge which meets in London called The White Swan Lodge No. 1348: <http://www.thewhiteswan.org/> [accessed the 12th of March, 2014]. The Grand Loge De France and the 'revived' Grand Lodge of All England had exchanged Treaties of Amity the previous year.

[257] Correspondence between the author and the Grand Master John Gordon Graves, dated the 29th of March, 2014.

[258] The Brethren of the 'revived' York Grand Lodge mentioned online were Grand Master John Gordon Graves; Grand Secretary Peter J. Clatworthy; Grand Chancellor Richard Martin Young and the first WM of the St John's Lodge in Dayton, Ohio, Daniel Scherr. There have been many independent Grand Lodges in the US that are not recognised by the regular Masonic bodies, and the 'revived' York Grand Lodge seems to have approached Freemasons for possible recruitment from this independent Masonic community; indeed, Scherr had previously been a member of two of these Grand Lodges in the US, and from correspondence between myself and Jeff Peace, an ex-Freemason from Georgia who was once linked to the independent Halcyon Lodge in Ohio, he recalled being approached by the 'revived' York Grand Lodge with an offer to join, but turned it down.

[259] See MQ, Issue 17, April 2006, UGLE Publications. <http://www.mqmagazine.co.uk/issue-17/p-05.php> [accessed the 12th of March, 2014]. Only two members are referred to as being involved.

constitution and its independent style. Perhaps when there is disagreement within Freemasonry, the old values of the York Grand Lodge are there to be examined, and its spirit will rise again, history repeating itself once more.

Appendix I

York Grand Lodge MS. No. 83.

This is a transcribed letter from Druidical member; wine and spirit dealer John Hassall to the Brethren of the York Grand Lodge, while Hassall was being held at York Castle due to debt in May 1780. It is a moving letter, not only because Hassall is desperately asking for relief, but as it reveals clues to the character of Hassall. He was poorly educated in comparison to the more intellectual Brethren of the York Grand Lodge such as the likes of John Browne, William Blanchard or Dr Francis Drake, but, he was a man of conviction and despite the letter having no mention in the York Grand Lodge minutes, the letter was endorsed by the Grand Secretary of the time John Browne, and it appears that relief was given and Hassall was released.

Hassall remained loyal to the York Grand Lodge, even when he moved to Manchester, founding a Royal Encampment of Knights Templar and of course, the Lodge of Fortitude in Hollinwood, revealing he was trusted and respected by the Grand Lodge. The letter has previously been transcribed by G.Y. Johnson in his 1942 work *The Subordinate Lodges*,[260] but this is a new transcription for this publication, in which I have had the assistance of Paul Booth MA, FR Hist. S. The spelling is the same as the original document, which was addressed 'For Mr John Brown Proctor in York'. The letter itself may have been written by someone else on Hassall's behalf as the rather rough Masonic symbol of the square and compass is marked by his name at the end of the letter, but either way, it was written by a 'semi-literate hand'.

Most Worthy Brothere   York Castle May 17 1780
I make bould to rite you to Lett you Noe I

I Ham in Great Distress at preasant my advrsarry as declare againt
me I would H Not Have trubled you but I cannot Healp it for I cannot
get Noe work to Done year and my wife is very ill and Cannot Healp me
at preasant So for God Sake you speak to mr Smith about me as Soon as
you can and in So doing I Shall be in Duty bound to pray for you all
I shall be Glad to See anny of you year So Noe more at preasant but Let
me year from as Soon as you Can from your Loving Brothere

John Hassall

---

[260] Johnson, *Subordinate Lodges*, p.67.

Appendix II

York Grand Lodge MS. No. 67

This is a transcribed letter written by the Master of Druidical Lodge; Attorney Josiah Beckwith, to the York Grand Lodge, dated the 23rd of October, 1779, regarding his visit to the Earl of Effingham on approaching him with the offer of the Office of Grand Master of the York Grand Lodge. A Peer of the Realm as Grand Master would have given the York Grand Lodge increased status and confidence, especially as the letter reveals the ongoing tensions between 'York' and the 'Modern' London based Grand Lodge, as the Earl was a 'Modern' Mason. It also brings to light how the *'Yorkites'* were firmly viewed as schismatics by the 'Moderns', a view that obviously angered the York Grand Lodge. The letter emphasises how one's social standing could be the main consideration for being offered the position of Grand Master within any English (and indeed Scottish or Irish) Grand Lodge at this time.

The letter also hints at how the York Grand Lodge may have approached members of the local gentry in a similar manner, with an intention of them becoming prominent members. Indeed, Effingham's friend and associate Hatfield Kay was also approached in an effort to influence the Earl, but despite being approved by the York Grand Lodge, Kay was never made a member. A reply was to be drafted to Beckwith, along with the *'Lodge of Antiquitys Manifesto'*, to give to Effingham, outlining the *'Unmasonick Conduct of the Nominal Grand Lodge in London'* in an attempt to put forward the York side of the story, suggesting that the Earl had been *'misinformed'* by the 'Moderns'. This reply also commented on the *'Unmasonic Distinction'* and *'Inconsistent Term'* used by the 'Moderns' of *'Ancient & Modern Masons'*, and puts forward that the 'Moderns', in disowning the 'Antients', have disowned their own origins, as they had actually originated from the *'Fraternity at the City of York'*.

However, despite their best efforts, Effingham subsequently turned down the offer, believing if he took up the position it may increase the friction between the York and 'Modern' Grand Lodges. For a Peer of the Realm who would have spent considerable time in London, he perhaps knew that 'defecting' to 'York' would have cut him off from visiting the lodges and fraternising with Freemasons under the 'Moderns'. Indeed, his Masonic career under the 'Moderns' would have abruptly ended and his move may have increased friction between the two rival Grand Lodges. The Earl later became the first Acting or Pro Grand Master of the 'Modern' Grand Lodge in 1782. The letter has previously been transcribed and discussed by G.Y. Johnson in his 1942 work *The Subordinate Lodges*.[261]

---

[261] Ibid., pp.52-8.

Sir, and Brother

After my respectful Compliments to the most worshipful Grand Master, and the Rest of the Brethren of the Grand Lodge of All England, I beg you will inform the Grand Lodge that I received the Resolution of the Committee, respecting an Application to our Right Honourable Brother, the Earl of Effingham; And That, in Consequence thereof, I took the first Opportunity of seeing his Lord-ship; which I could not do till last Night, owing to his Lordship's having been from Home.

His Lordship received me as a Brother, with all the Marks of Cordiality, Brotherly Love, true Politeness and Affability possible; and desired that I would, in his Name, thank the Brethren of the Grand Lodge for the very distinguishing Mark of Honour they meant to confer upon him, by electing him their Grand Master; an Honour his Lordship would accept, with great Pleasure, if he could be satisfied that, by so doing, the Interests of Maceonry in general would be promoted.—But his Lordship fears that it would be attended with a quite contrary Effect, and that it would be a Means of widening the Breach between the Grand Lodge of All England, and the Grand Lodge of England, which acknowledges the Duke of Manchester for Grand Master.

His Lordship is past Master of a Lodge under the latter Constitution, and therefore thinks he should act derogatorily to his Obligation should he accept of the Dignity of Grand Master of the Antient York Maceons: his Lordship being a Modern one: tho' his Lordship utterly dislikes the Distinction of Antient and Modern, says we differ in Forms only, and not in Essentials, and ought all to agree together.

His Lordship says he abhorrs the Thoughts of Tyrany in any Set of Men,[262] and Particularly Maceons, and, if he is satisfied that the Grand Lodge of England has behaved improperly to the Grand Lodge at York, he will oblige them to make proper Acknowledgments for it; and will use his utmost Endeavours to promote a Reconciliation between the two Lodges, when he goes to London.

His Lordship added, with that nobleness of Thought and Expression which characterises the true old English Patriot, that he would sacrifice his Purse, his Limbs, nay even his Life to promote the true Interests of Maceonry; which he looked upon to be the noblest Institution in the World.

I told his Lordship that, for my own Part, I was a very young Maceon; that I did not think myself equal to the Task of explaining to his Lordship the Benefits that might accrue to Maceonry, in General, by his Lordship's Acceptance of the Dignity of Grand Master; tho' I was well satisfied in my own Mind that it would have that Operation; but that I had no Doubt but some of my Brethren at York, who had Opportunities of knowing, and knew much more than I did, could

---

[262] Indeed, Effingham was against Britain's policy in the American War of Independence.

satisfy his Lordship of the Utility of his Lordship's Acceptance of that Dignity; and would, I durst say, not think it any Trouble to wait upon his Lordship for that Purpose, if his Lordship would permit them so to do. His Lordship replied that no Person needed any other Introduction to him than that of being a Maceon; and was pleased to give a General Invitation to myself, and any of the Brethren who would take the Trouble of waiting upon him, (to use his own Phrase,) to see how his Mutton was roasted.

I think I have given you a Detail of the Substance of what passed between me and his Lordship, with whom I spent about an Hour. His Lordship's Behaviour was, upon the whole, uncommonly generous and affable, and I am of Opinion that if a few of the Brethren from York would not think it too much Trouble to come over and wait upon his Lordship at the Grange, before he attends Parliament, that their Representation of Matters to him would be attended with very desirable Consequences to the Grand Lodge, even if his Lordship should still decline the Office of Grand Master.

We had a Lodge last Night, at the Time when his Lordship was in the Town, but his Lordship declined attending as a visiting Brother, for that Time; tho' he gave us Hopes that he would Join us e'er long.

I find his Lordship has had Matters represented to him by the Grand Lodge of England, in their own Way, and looks upon us as Schismatics; and I therefore wish that he had a true State of the Dispute laid before him: which I am not Master enough of the Subject to do as it ought to be done.

His Lordship told me that he always made it a Rule, when in London, to attend a Lodge once a Week, or once a Fortnight at the furthest.

All the Brethren here, Greet the Brethren at York with Brotherly Love, and I am

        Sir,

P.S.

If you should find it necessary to write
To me, during the Course of the ensuing
Week, please to direct your Letter to
Me at the Red Lyon in Doncaster;
Where I shall be upon a Commision.

}

Your affectionate Brother, and
Very humble Servant
Josiah Beckwith.
Rotherham, 23. October 1779.

Appendix III

Some leading members of the York Grand Lodge visited the York 'Union' Lodge during the opening years of the nineteenth century; the Rev. John Parker - the Grand Chaplain, led the way attending around 25 times between 1802-1814. Accompanying the good Reverend on separate occasions was Robert Sinclair, the last known Grand Master Edward Wolley, and another possible York Grand Lodge visitor was Joseph Ryder Reynoldson. Recognisable family names of old York Grand Lodge stalwarts can also be seen joining the 'Union' Lodge such as Francis Agar and John Bewlay.

What is an interesting factor however was that the Rev. Parker regularly attended under the title of *Grand Chaplain of All England*, with Edward Wolley also being mentioned as a member of the Grand Lodge of All England when he visited. This is not only interesting in light of the general historical consensus that the York Grand Lodge ended in 1792, but shows that the York Grand Lodge was still respected in the York based 'Modern' lodge and that being a member was still important enough to use in the Masonic context. Below is a list of the entries of the attendance by the Rev. John Parker, Edward Wolley and Robert Sinclair, as taken from the York 'Union' Lodge No. 236 minute books from the period; Minute Books 10 and 11.

10th of March 1802: **The Rev. John Parker's** first appearance, were he gives a discourse for the death of Brother Dunn. Parker was referred to as Grand Chaplain.

1st of June 1802: **The Rev. John Parker** visits again and is referred to as Grand Chaplain. **Bro. Sinclair** honours the lodge with his presence.

27th of August 1802: **The Rev. John Parker** and **Edward Wolley** both visited, both being referred to as members of the Grand Lodge of All England.

18th of October 1802: *'Joseph Ryder Reynoldson of the ancient Grand Lodge'* visited, who may be the same Joseph Reynoldson who was a member of the York Grand Lodge.

1st of November 1802: Joseph Ryder Reynoldson visited again.

21st of June 1803: **The Rev. Parker** visited as Grand Chaplain.

19th of September 1803: **The Rev. Parker** again visited Grand Chaplain.

21st of December 1803: **The Rev. Parker** visited but was not listed as Grand Chaplain.

25th of June 1804: **The Rev. Parker** visited but was not listed as Grand Chaplain.

24th of June 1805: **The Rev. Parker** visited but was not listed as Grand Chaplain.

2nd of September 1805: **The Rev. Parker** visited but was not listed as Grand Chaplain.

16th of September 1805: **The Rev. Parker** visited and was listed as Grand Chaplain.

7th of October 1805: **The Rev. Parker** again visited and was listed as Grand Chaplain.

15th of October 1805: **The Rev. Parker** again visited and was listed as Grand Chaplain.

16th of December 1805: It was proposed that a funeral procession for Admiral Nelson by the lodge should take place, with **The Rev. Parker** giving a sermon. The procession 'hatchment' still survives and is on display at Duncombe Place in York.

21st of April 1806: **The Rev. Parker** visited and was referred to as Grand Chaplain.

16th of June 1806: **The Rev. Parker** visited and was referred to as Grand Chaplain.

7th of July 1806: **The Rev. Parker** visited and was referred to as Grand Chaplain.

26th of June 1809: **The Rev Parker** visited and was referred to Grand Chaplain of All England.

27th of December 1809: **The Rev. Parker** visited and is referred to as Grand Chaplain.

2nd of June 1810: **The Rev. Parker** visited and is referred to as Grand Chaplain.

27th of November 1810: **The Rev. Parker** visited and is referred to only as Chaplain.

27th of December 1811: **The Rev. Parker** visited and is referred to only as Chaplain.

24th of June 1812: **The Rev. Parker** visited and is referred to only as Chaplain.

24th of June 1813: **The Rev. Parker** visited and is referred to only as Chaplain.

27th of December 1813: **The Rev. Parker** appeared as a visitor.

7th of July 1814: The final appearance of the **Rev. Parker** giving a sermon after the lodge procession.

Appendix IV

Freemason members of the Good Humour Club

The Good Humour Club operated from c.1725-1800 and met at Sunton's Coffee House, Coney Street, York. There were a number of club members who were also members of the 'Modern' Apollo Lodge, which also met at a residence on Coney Street; the George Inn. Founders of Apollo were ex-members of the York Grand Lodge. Research was undertaken by Hugh Murray for the Laurence Sterne Trust in 2013.

Ricard	C	Member of Lodge 259 1761-3. Mar June 1746.*
Tasker	Jonathan	Silk Mercer Stonegate, member of Lodge 259 1761-3
Oldfield	Joshua	Wine Merchant Lendal 1738-96 Free 1763 LM 1790 VP.* Rockingham Club, member of Apollo Lodge 1773.
Camidge	John	1734-1803 Organist York Minster 1756-99 mar 1796. Member of Apollo Lodge in 1777, Master in 1780.
Johnson	William	Clergyman, member of Apollo Lodge 1777.
Braint	Joseph	Butter Factor w/o Micklegte Bar in p'ship with R Garland. 1784 Merchant. Founder member of Apollo Lodge in 1773.
Frobisher	Nathaniel	Stationer, member of Apollo Lodge in 1777.
Garland	Richard	Butter Factor Goodramgate in p'ship with J Braint 1784 Merchant. Founder member of Apollo Lodge in 1773.
Sinclair	Robert	Joined York Grand Lodge in 1766. Also visited the Apollo Lodge.

* Tasker and Ricard joined the York Grand Lodge; Lodge 259 becoming known as the Punch Bowl Lodge.

Bibliography

There are numerous publications regarding the York Grand Lodge; from a detailed mention by R.F. Gould in his *History of Freemasonry*, with various papers in *AQC* and the *MAMR*, references made in various Masonic Encyclopaedias, to the more recent work of Neville Barker Cryer, a Yorkshire based Masonic historian, who wrote the more recent *York Mysteries Revealed*. This book, which is essential reading, was self published in 2006 and includes a detailed account of the York Grand Lodge, although there is a distinct lack of referencing and, as previously mentioned, a rather sensationalist foreword by Michael Baigent.

Special reference should be made to G.Y. Johnson, once the Librarian of the York 'Union' Lodge and member of QC Lodge who transcribed many York Grand Lodge documents and catalogued them. Johnson's excellent work *The Subordinate Lodges Constituted by the York Grand Lodge* presented transcriptions of the documents associated with the lodges under the sway of York and discussed their role within the York Grand Lodge administration. Essential reading can also be found with Poole and Worts' *"Yorkshire" Old Charges of Masons* which offers an exceptional analysis of the Old Charges held at York, including the York MS No. 1. My previous work on the York Grand Lodge can be found in Chapter 9 of my first book *The Genesis of Freemasonry*, which looks at the York Grand Lodge as a staunchly independent Grand Lodge.

There is still a lot to see in York regarding the Grand Lodge; the elegant town houses of past York members such as Fairfax House and the house of Charles Bathurst at Micklegate, the Merchant Adventurers' Hall which of course was the location for Drake's famous speech in 1726, the Punch Bowl is well worth a visit, and of course the artefacts and manuscripts held at Duncombe Place. Fairfax House and the Merchant Adventurers' Hall are open to the public.

Primary Source Material
The main source material that still exists on the York Grand Lodge can be located at Duncombe Place in York, and there are certain other existing lodges that hold York artefacts. The York Grand Lodge documents, which date periodically from the 19th of March, 1712 and end on the 23rd of August, 1792, are in the possession of the York 'Union' Lodge No.236. The first collection of records begin on the 19th of March, 1712 and end on the 4th of May, 1730, and are to be found on a parchment roll known as Roll No. 7. There is a mention of an '*Original Minute Book of this* (the York) *Grand Lodge*' which dated from 1705-1734, in a letter dated August 1778 from the Grand Secretary Jacob Bussey, to Bro. B. Bradley of the Lodge of Antiquity in London.

There are no minutes at all between the years 1734-1761 and a possible earlier document listing earlier meetings from 1705-1712 has disappeared. Other York Grand Lodge relics, including furniture, jewels, manuscript rolls including the various Antient Charges, the rule dating from 1663, collective letters and the original Warrant for the Lodge of Fortitude, are all held at Freemasons Hall, Duncombe Place, York, which is the current residence of the York 'Union' Lodge. There are also an excellent collection of books held at Duncombe Place, dating from the eighteenth and early nineteenth centuries, such as the rare copy of William Preston's *Illustrations of Masonry*, and an original copy of Drake's *Eboracum*.

The minutes of the revived York Grand Lodge are also held at Duncombe Place by the York 'Union' Lodge No. 236. Johnson and Bramwell comprehensively catalogued the lodge's library in 1958; there are the two York Grand Lodge minute books covering 1761-1774 and 1774-1780, and the two York Grand Lodge Royal Arch minute books covering 1762-1772 and 1778-1781 respectively. There is a list of members (MS Roll No. 10) that includes all initiates from 1761-1790 and a scrap of paper that has a manuscript minute from 23rd August 1792. QC member Thomas B. Whytehead (WM in 1899), who was also editor of the *Yorkshire Gazette*, wrote several articles about the Grand Lodge of All England at York and concluded that a minute book probably existed covering the period 1782-1792 but its existence was unknown (AQC Vol. 13, p.93-123). All subsequent research into the Grand Lodge of All England has reached a similar conclusion. There are also the lists of members & minutes of the Lodge of Friendship, No.277, dating from 1789, once based in Oldham, but now located at the Rochdale Masonic Hall. The minutes and artefacts of the Jerusalem Preceptory No. 5 are held at the Manchester Masonic Hall.

Source Material relating to the York Grand Lodge currently held at the UGLE
The material relating to the York Grand Lodge can be found on the UGLE catalogue by doing a subject search for "Grand Lodge of All England, York". This includes the Francis Drake speech from 1726. There is also the following:

· A manuscript certificate dated 15th January 1768 for Sir Walter Vavasour, Baronet signed by the Grand Mater (George Palmes), SGW, JGW and Grand Secretary of the Grand Lodge of All England at York. Ironically Vavasour eventually became a Provincial Grand Master of Yorkshire for the London based 'Modern' Grand Lodge in 1780 but resigned in 1783 when he realised they actually wanted him to attend meetings.

· A blank summons/certificate featuring the crypt of York Minster above some interesting Masonic symbols including pyramids and Noah's Ark resting on Mount Ararat, by the engraver and artist Thomas Beckwith. Bernard Jones in his

"Freemasons' book of the Royal Arch" equates this summons with York 'Union' Lodge, No. 236 but it matches the design of the York Grand Lodge board which is now in their possession, and Gilbert Johnson in "Some notes on the York Grand Lodge" (1947) mentions that Thomas Beckwith was a member of the York Grand Lodge, though he doesn't appear to know about the summons. According to Johnson, Beckwith, who was also an antiquarian, wrote several (unpublished) volumes on York history and he includes some of Beckwith's passages about the York Grand Lodge in his article. A substantial amount of Beckwith's papers are held in collection by the Yorkshire Archaeological Society (http://www.yas.org.uk) Ref: MS60-79.

·There is also a manuscript book called "[Rules and orders, discretionary by-laws, laws respecting the R. A. sick fund, rules and orders of the R. A. Chapter, list of marks]" for the Lodge of Fortitude, Hollinwood; the last known lodge warranted by the Grand Lodge of All England at York in 1790. This is shelved at BE 167 FOR. This is a very interesting little note book which includes the By-laws for the lodge, the Royal Arch, a sick fund and has evidence of Mark Masonry, but interestingly also has extracts from Thomas Smith Webb's *Freemason's Monitor* which was not published until 1797 in the US. The date of 1802 is given in the book, the compiler having copied from Webb's 1802 New York edition. This note book is mentioned by Masonic historian Fred Pick in *MAMR*, Vol. LIII, (1963), p.37.

Other documents relating to Dr Francis Drake
Drake, Francis (1696-1771) Antiquary 163085
Antiquary Francis Drake miscellaneous papers relating to Civil War letters to Dr Charles Lyttelton, letters to Sir Hans Sloane, miscellaneous correspondence, and notes on Dodsworth collection miscellaneous correspondence letters (25) to him and Caesar Ward from Charles Lyttelton History of York. Date range: 1696-1771. Source: National Register of Archives (NRA, local and private archives).

Society of Antiquaries. 'Register Book of the Society of Antiquaries of London'
Lethieullier (SAL/MS/264 B, pp. 91-2). Minute Book II, 12 Feb. 1735/6, pp.148-9. fol. 51r, v;- (14) Introduction by Francis Drake, FSA, to the MS discourse on heraldic seals by John Anstis, the elder, Garter 'Aspilogia sive de Iconibus Scutariis'; Date range: 1735 - 1753. Source: Access to Archives (A2A): not kept at The National Archives.

Published Primary Source Material
Anderson, James, *The Constitutions of The Free-Masons*, (London: Senex, 1723).

Anderson, James, *The New Book of Constitutions of the Antient and Honourable Fraternity of Free and Accepted Masons*, (London: Ward and Chandler, 1738).

Anderson, James, *The Constitutions of the Antient and Honourable Fraternity of Free and Accepted Masons, Revised by John Entick MA*, (London: J. Scott, 1756).

Anderson, James, *Constitutions of the Antient and Honourable Fraternity of Free and Accepted Masons*, (London: G. Kearsly, 1769).

Anon., *The Antient Constitutions of the Free and Accepted Masons, with a speech deliver'd at the Grand Lodge at York*, (London: B. Creake, 1731).

Anon., *Three Distinct Knocks*, (London, 1760).

Anon., *Jachin and Boaz; or an Authentic Key To the Door of Free-Masonry, Both Antient and Modern*, (London: W. Nicoll, St. Paul's Church-Yard, 1763).

Dermott, Laurence, *Ahiman Rezon*, (London, 1756).

Dermott, Laurence, *Ahiman Rezon, or a help to all that are, or would be Free and Accepted Masons, Second Edition*, (London: Sold by Br. Robert Black, 1764).

Dermott, Laurence, *Ahiman Rezon or a Help to all that are, or would be Free and Accepted Masons (with many additions), Third Edition*, (London: Printed for James Jones, 1778).

Drake, Francis, *Eboracum or The History and Antiquities of the City of York, from its Original to the Present Time; together with the History of the Cathedral Church and the Lives of the Archbishops of that See*, (London: William Bowyer, 1736).

Drake, Francis, *Eboracum*, (York: Wilson and Spence, 1788).

Hargrove, William, *History and Description of the Ancient City of York: comprising all the most interesting information already published in Drake's Eboracum*, (York: William Alexander, 1818).

Paine, Thomas, *The Works of Thomas Paine*, (New York: E. Haskell, 1854).

Parker, John, Vicar of St. Helen's York, *A sermon, preached in the parish-church of Rotherham, before the Most Worshipful Grand Master of the most ancient Grand Lodge of all England ... and the newly constituted Rotherham Druidical Lodge of Free and Accepted Masons, December 22, 1778*, (York: W. Blanchard and Co., 1779).

Preston, William, *Illustrations of Masonry*, (London: Whittaker, Treacher & Co., 1829).

Ramsden Riley, J., *The Yorkshire Lodges: A Century of Yorkshire Freemasonry*, (Leeds: Thomas C. Jack, 1885).

Smith, Joseph, *A Descriptive Catalogue of Friends' Books, or Books written by the Members of the Society of Friends, commonly called Quakers*, (London: Joseph Smith, 1867).

Sterne, Laurence, *The Life and Opinions of Tristram Shandy, Gentleman*, (London: R. & J. Dodsley, 1760).

Timperley, Charles Henry, *A Dictionary of Printers and Printing*, (London: Johnson, 1839).

Webb, Thomas Smith, *Webb's Freemason's Monitor*, (Cincinnati: C. Moore, 1865).

Wilkinson, Tate, *Memoirs of His own Life*, (York: Wilson, Spence and Mawman, 1790).

Wilkinson, Tate, *The Wandering Patentee, Or A History of the Yorkshire Theatres From 1770 to the Present Time*, (York: Wilson, Spence and Mawman, 1795).

The theatrical inquisitor, or, Monthly mirror, Volume 12, (London: C. Chapple, 1818).

Burials for St. Mary's Church, Oldham, Jonathan Raynor, 14th of April, 1811, Source Film No. 1656225, Ref No. 6.

Lodge Histories
Brown, J., *Masonry in Wigan being a brief history of the Lodge of Antiquity No. 178, Wigan, originally No. 235*, (Wigan: R. Platt, Standishgate and Millgate, 1882).

Crossley, Herbert, *The History of the Lodge of Probity No. 61*, (Hull: M.C. Peck & Son, 1888).

Morton, Albert, *A Brief History of Freemasonry in Richmond, Yorkshire, Compiled from the records of the Lennox Lodge, No. 123, and other sources*, (Richmond: Thomas Spencer, 1911).

Morton, Albert, *Lennox Lodge, No. 123*, (Richmond: 1947).

F.C. Shepherd & M.P. Lane, *Jerusalem Preceptory No. 5. Bi-Centenary History 1786-1986*, (Manchester: Published privately by the Preceptory, 1986).

Wood, Robert Leslie, *York Lodge No. 236, formerly The Union Lodge, the be-centennial history 1777-1977*, (York: Published privately by the lodge, 1977).

Secondary Sources
Armstrong, John, *History of Freemasonry in Cheshire*, (London: Kenning, 1901).

Ayres, Philip J., *Classical Culture and the Idea of Rome in Eighteenth-Century England*, (Cambridge: Cambridge University Press, 1997).

Barker Cryer, Neville, *Masonic Halls of England The North*, (Shepperton: Lewis Masonic, 1989).

Barker Cryer, Neville, *York Mysteries Revealed*, (Hersham: Barker Cryer, 2006).

Benson, G., *John Browne 1793-1877, Artist and the Historian of York Minster.* (York: Yorkshire Philosophical Society, 1918).

Gould, Robert Freke, *History of Freemasonry*, Vol.I-III, (London: Thomas C. Jack, 1883).

Gould, Robert Freke, *The Concise History of Freemasonry*, (New York: Dover Publications, 2007).

Harrison, David, *The Genesis of Freemasonry*, (Hersham: Lewis Masonic, 2009).

Harrison, David, *The Transformation of Freemasonry*, (Bury St. Edmunds: Arima Publishing, 2010).

Harrison, David, *The Liverpool Masonic Rebellion and the Wigan Grand Lodge*, (Bury St. Edmunds: Arima Publishing, 2012).

Hughan, William James, *The Old Charges of British Freemasons*, (London: Simpkin, Marshall and Co., 1872).

Johnson, G.Y., *The Subordinate Lodges Constituted by the York Grand Lodge*, (Margate: W.J. Parrett, Reprinted from AQC Vols. LII and LIII, 1942).

Knoop, D., and Jones, G.P., *A Short History Of Freemasonry To 1730,* (Manchester: Manchester University Press, 1940).

Knoop, D., and Jones, G.P., (ed.), *Early Masonic Pamphlets*, (Manchester: University of Manchester Press, 1945).

Knoop, D., and Jones, G.P., *The Genesis of Freemasonry*, (Manchester: University of Manchester Press, 1947).

Knoop, D., and Jones, G.P., *The Mediaeval Mason: An Economic History of English Stone Building in the Later Middle Ages and Early Modern Times*, (New York: Barnes and Noble, 1967).

Mackenzie, Kenneth, *The Royal Masonic Cyclopaedia*, (Wellingborough: The Antiquarian Press, 1987).

Maclean, Fitzroy, *Bonnie Prince Charlie*, (Edinburgh: Canongate, 1989).

McKeown, Trevor W., 'An historical outline of freemasons online', Grand Lodge of British Columbia and Yukon, (2008).

Poole, H., and Worts, F.R., *"Yorkshire" Old Charges of Masons*, (York: Ben Johnson & Co. Ltd, 1935).

Porter, Roy, *Enlightenment*, (London: Penguin, 2000).

Rogers, Norman, *Two Hundred Years of Freemasonry in Bolton*, (MAMR, 1941).

Rosenfeld, Sybil, *Strolling Players and Drama in the Provinces 1660-1765*, (Cambridge: Cambridge University Press, 1939).

Springett, Bernard H., *The Mark Degree*, (London: A. Lewis, 1968).

Waite, Arthur Edward, *Secret Tradition in Freemasonry*, (Kessinger, 1997).

Journals

Dunn, P.M., 'Dr John Burton (1710-1771) of York and his obstetric treatise', in *Arch Dis Child Fetal Neonatal*, 84, (2001).

Gilbert, R.A., 'The Masonic Career of A.E. Waite', in *AQC*, Vol.99, (1986).

Harrison, David, 'Freemasonry, Industry and Charity: The Local Community and the Working Man'. *JIVR*, Volume 5, Number 1, (Winter 2002), pp.33-45.

Harrison, David and Belton, John, 'Society in Flux' in *Researching British Freemasonry 1717-2017: JCRFF*, Vol. 3, (Sheffield: University of Sheffield, 2010), pp.71-99.

Harrison, David, 'The Liverpool Masonic rebellion and the Grand Lodge of Wigan', in *THSLC*, Vol. 160, (2012), pp.67-88.

Harrison, David, 'The Lymm Freemasons; A New Insight into Transition-Era Freemasonry', in *Heredom*, Vol. 19, (Washington: Scottish Rite Research Society, 2011), pp.169-190.

Harrison, David, 'The Last Years of the York Grand Lodge – Part One', in *The Journal of the Masonic Society*, the Masonic Society, Issue 23, (Winter, 2014), pp.16-23.

Pick, Fred L., 'Lodge of Friendship No. 277; A Link With The Grand Lodge Of All England, At York', *MAMR*, Vol.XXI, (1931), pp.149-154.

Pick, Fred L., 'The Lodge of Friendship No. 277 With Notes on Some Neighbouring Lodges and Chapters', *MAMR*, Vol. XXIII, (1933), pp.74-123.

Pick, Fred L., 'The Lodge of Fortitude at Hollinwood', *MAMR*, Vol. LIII, (1963), pp.32-7.

Pound, Ricky, 'Chiswick House - a Masonic Temple?', in Gillian Clegg (eds.), *Brentford & Chiswick Local History Journal*, Number 16, 2007, pp.4-7.

Raine, J, (ed.), Fabric Rolls of York Minster (1360-1639, with an Appendix, 1165-1704), Surtees Society, Vol. 35, (London: Mitchell and Son, 1859).

Rogers, Norman, 'The Lodge of Sincerity, No. 1 of the Wigan Grand Lodge', *AQC*, Vol. LXII, (1951), pp.33-76.

Rylands, W.H., 'Freemasonry in Lancashire & Cheshire in the 17th Century', *LCHS*, (1898), pp.131-202.

Sweet, Rosemary, 'History and Identity in Eighteenth-Century York: Francis Drake's *Eboracum* (1736)', in *Eighteenth-Century York: Culture, Space and Society*, (York: University of York, 2003), pp.14-23.

Whytehead, T.B., 'The Relics of the Grand Lodge at York', in *AQC*, Vol. XIII, (1900), pp.93-115.

Online Sources
<http://www.markmastermasonscornwall.org.uk/history-of-mark-master-masons> [accessed 30th of May, 2012]

'Newspapers', A History of the County of York: the City of York (1961), pp.537-541.   URL: <http://www.british-history.ac.uk/report.aspx?compid=36391> [accessed: 19th of May 2012]

Lane's Masonic Records <http://freemasonry.dept.shef.ac.uk/lane/> [accessed 9th of June, 2012]

<http://www.brad.ac.uk/webofhiram/?section=york_rite&page=grandyork.html> [accessed 1st of February, 2013]

C.J. Scott, *The Tradition of The Old York T. I. Lodge of Mark Master Masons: An enquiry into early Freemasonry at Bradford and neighborhood 1713-1873*. A paper given before the Old York T.I. Lodge at Bradford on November 28th, 1911.

<http://www.bradford.ac.uk/webofhiram/?section=york_rite&page=tradoldyork.html> [accessed 30th of October, 2013]

Index

Lightning Source UK Ltd.
Milton Keynes UK
UKOW04f0041270614

234112UK00001B/4/P